JOE TORRE'S
GROUND RULES FOR WINNERS

JOE
GROUND RULES

12 Keys to
Managing
Team Players,
Tough Bosses,
Setbacks, and
Success

TORRE'S
FOR WINNERS

JOE TORRE
with Henry Dreher

HYPERION
NEW YORK

Designed by Ruth Lee

ISBN: 0-7868-6568-7

FIRST EDITION

10 9 8 7 6 5 4 3 2 1

To my motivator, my wife, Ali.

To my daughter, Andrea—
my reason for enjoying every single day on earth.

And to my older children,
Michael, Lauren, and Christina.
                    —Joe Torre

For my wife, Deborah,
whose love and support has been my key.
                    —Henry Dreher

Contents

CONTENTS

Acknowledgments

I thank George Steinbrenner for bringing me to the Yankees, and Arthur Richman for whispering in George's ear. This book would not have been possible otherwise.

—JOE TORRE

We both wish to thank our agent, Jonathan Diamond, as well as Bob Rosen, Maury Gostfrand, and Chris Tomasino of RLR Associates. They did a great job in all phases of this project. We thank Rick Cerrone of the Yankees for his valuable assistance. We are grateful to many people at Hyperion, most especially our editor, Gretchen Young, for her thoughtful guidance and enthusiasm; Jennifer Morgan; Martha Levin; Jodi Glaser-Taub; David Lott; and Bob Miller for his commitment to this book from the very start.

—JOE TORRE AND HENRY DREHER

I wish to thank my wife, Deborah Chiel, for her invaluable counsel as I worked on this book. I am also indebted to certain people for their moral support: Rena Borow, Michael Fox, Daniel Chiel, and Jesse Krotick.

—HENRY DREHER

JOE TORRE'S
GROUND RULES FOR WINNERS

Introduction

On the eve of the New York Yankees' 1998 World Series triumph, I was having dinner with my wife, Ali, when I asked a question that sometimes pops into my head about my recent good fortune in baseball. "Why me?"

I asked this question because I could not fully grasp my good luck. When George Steinbrenner hired me to manage the Yankees in 1996, I had been in baseball for over three decades as a player and manager. I had never once been to the World Series without buying a ticket. I had hardly ever come close. I had just been fired from my job as manager of the St. Louis Cardinals, the third firing in my fifteen-year managerial career. I thought I would never manage again.

Here it was, October 1998, and I was on the verge of steering the Yankees to their second world championship in three years. My team had broken the American League record for most wins in a season. The next day we would complete a sweep of the San Diego Padres, to finish the year with a record of 125–50. No baseball team had ever won 125 games. I had been privileged to lead a remarkable group of men. They played the entire season with dedication, professionalism, and relentless passion. These guys had more heart than any group I had ever seen.

Why me? Why did George Steinbrenner pick me when I thought my career had been finished? I wondered if the good Lord didn't think I could appreciate my blessings until now. But I also thought about my entire career in baseball—how I had gotten to this moment, and what it all meant. I had become a manager because I love baseball and felt that I had leadership skills. When I came so close to the end of my managing career, I thought perhaps it wasn't meant to be. But my success with the Yankees helped me to realize what I have to offer as a leader. I've had to acknowledge that my success occurred for a reason: my philosophy and beliefs worked. My years of dedication, learning, and growing had paid off. I know that I was fortunate to have a great group of players in both championship seasons of 1996 and 1998, and when we came up short in 1997. No manager can win without players. Yet it was a perfect match, one that allowed me to make the best use of my knowledge, skills, and judgment with people.

Why me? Perhaps I was not only lucky, but I was also being rewarded for doing something right, for sticking to principles of management I had believed in throughout my career.

I decided to write *Ground Rules for Winners* to share my philosophy of management and motivation. I have broken it down into a series of twelve simple "keys" that anyone can follow to become a more effective team player, manager, or executive. I know that these keys work, because they represent everything I have put into practice in my four years as skipper of the Yankees. I have seen players raise their game, and my team as a whole perform at a level of excellence no one would have imagined.

The twelve keys have worked for me, and I am certain they will work for any executive or manager in the corporate world. They offer as much to employees—the "team players" at all levels of an organization. For instance, Key #2 teaches fairness, respect, and trust as the basis for productive business relationships. These are lessons for everyone, since both managers and employees need to offer each other fairness, respect, and trust. It's always a two-way street.

I tell kids and young players at every level that winning is a by-product of getting the most out of your ability. Don't stop believing in yourself because you haven't yet been rewarded with that brass ring. If I had stopped believing in myself, I never would have been able to guide a great team to its great accomplishments. I never would have realized my lifelong dream of making it to the World Series. It took me 4,272 games as a player and a manager to finally get there, the longest wait for anyone in the history of the game.

Given this background, I can safely say that I understand the value of patience, optimism, and commitment. It's why I can tell people to hold on to their dreams and convictions without sounding like a walking cliché. I also have come to understand how we can remain positive and calm in the face of short- and long-term setbacks. The twelve keys give you practical ways to deal with the toughest obstacles you'll face as a manager or team player.

I teach not only how to handle setbacks, but also success. In my opening speech at spring training in 1999, I told my players not to measure themselves against the year before. Someone will break Mark McGwire's home-run record long before a team wins 126 games. "Don't shoot for the same record," I said. "Just shoot for the same preparation." As the 1999 season continues, it has not been easy for my team to deal with the pressure of so much success. It took almost half a season before they seemed to leave behind comparisons to their record-breaking '98 season.

Ground Rules for Winners also includes a complete section on dealing with tough bosses. I have had my share of tough bosses as a manager, including George Steinbrenner, principal owner of the Yankees. George's reputation preceded him, yet we have developed a most productive and satisfying work relationship—one that has contributed to the Yankees' success. People ask, "How did you do that?" I provide answers in this section, and I use my experiences as the basis for practical advice on how anyone can work effectively with a tough boss.

During spring training of 1999, I was diagnosed with prostate cancer. This time I did not ask the question, "Why me?" The only question I have considered is "Why not me?" Some people are going to get this disease, and I don't see why I should be exempt. Sandy Koufax called me at home after my diagnosis, and I jokingly said, "Now I know why all those bloop singles fell in last year."

I have tried to remain philosophical about my diagnosis, but I have also been frightened and had quite a few sleepless nights. But I've learned that many of the keys to handling

Introduction

challenges at work are just as valuable in life. Serenity, optimism, resilience, steadiness, and commitment are among the
qualities I have tried to sustain. I hope that anyone with a
serious illness will find some strength and comfort in my
advice on how to deal with setbacks.

It's been very gratifying that the philosophy I have
always held dear has been acknowledged for its effectiveness.
It represents the values I cherish—respect, trust, integrity, and
commitment to our work and the people with whom we
share our lives. I offer it here in the hope that it will enable
you to realize dreams you never thought possible.

CHAPTER 1 **Key #1:**

Know Your Team Players

What is success? Is success winning? Cutting the deal? Maximizing profits? Collecting awards? Winning the ball game? Capturing the championship?

Depending on your line of work, success can be any or all of these things. But in my book, success and winning are not always one and the same. Perhaps it will seem odd that here I am insisting, in a book called *Ground Rules for Winners,* that you can succeed without winning. To me, success is playing—or working—to the best of your ability. And *winning* is a by-product of living up to your highest standards for yourself, getting the most out of your natural talents, reaching down and rooting out your own drive, courage, and commitment. In other words, if you succeed in realizing your own abilities, the chances that you'll be a winner in objective terms—with all the rewards—are maximized.

Don't get me wrong, winning is a valid goal. It is the pot of gold at the end of the journey, no matter how short (one game) or long (a whole season or year). But success should be your daily focus. You can't win every day, but you can succeed in fulfilling your potential as an individual and a team member.

That's why baseball is such a perfect metaphor for life. In football, for example, a season of sixteen wins and no losses is conceivable—it's been done. In baseball, you're considered a wild success if you lose fewer than 60 games in one season. In 1998, my players, coaches, and I woke up with that gnawing feeling of defeat on *fifty* mornings, yet this was the year in which we broke the major league record for most victories (125) in a season. Baseball's 162-game schedule—the "grind" I have known for thirty-two years—is in fact much closer to the daily lives of most people. You get up every morning, do your best, make small steps forward, suffer setbacks that obscure your long-term progress, fight off hassles and absurd obstacles, and once in a blue moon, you actually achieve a cherished goal that's been the stuff of your dreams. Then, with the world's permission, you can call yourself a winner. But only you know how many small triumphs and snarls went into that big victory, how many months, years, or decades of sweat and sorrow preceded that breakthrough. That's baseball, and that's life.

My belief that success and winning are not one and the same may buck current trends in motivational thinking. But I speak largely from my own experience, as a player and manager who has played 4,272 games before making it to the World Series. As a manager prior to coming to the Yankees, my win-loss record was 119 games below .500. If in my own mind and heart I had defined success purely as winning, I might have seen myself as a failure. Although I've had periods of self-doubt, and times when I did not live up to my own high expectations, I never gave in to the idea that I was somehow a failure. Had I done so, I might have completely stopped believing in myself and the possibility of realizing my dream—a World Series championship as a player or manager.

Why should you distinguish between success and winning? First, you don't want to hang your whole identity on the hook of winning. If you do, you could totally sabotage yourself. In a team sport—and in life, for that matter—you can maximize your talents and still lose because you lack the teammates or resources or commitment from upper management that give you the best shot at winning. In all my years as a manager with the Mets, Braves, and Cardinals, I never had the "horses," as top-flight players are called, to help get our team to the big dance. I never fell for the illusion that I'd done a perfect job. Nor did I blame others. I simply made a realistic assessment of my situation, and concluded that it wasn't all my fault. I refused to write myself off as a major league manager with the potential to win a world championship. I wasn't sure it would ever happen, but I knew that I had the ability to make it, given the right circumstances. Once you brand yourself a loser, you'll never maintain the level of drive and optimism necessary to keep working hard, to pursue your goals with unwavering passion and intensity.

Second, if you're a player who focuses on realizing *your* abilities, or a manager who focuses on helping your team players to realize *their* abilities, you've got your priorities straight. Rather than living and dying by your latest win-loss record, or whether you've made it to the top of the heap that year, you concentrate on the day-to-day realities of being the best you can be—as an individual and a team member.

How do you make it happen? As an individual, you work relentlessly on the fundamentals of the game—whatever your game may be. In baseball, that means honing your fielding skills, making smart adjustments at the plate, and practicing basics like bunting, hitting behind the runner, and baserunning. In business, it may mean developing an outstanding prospectus, crunching numbers correctly, or perfecting the art of the deal. As a team member, you care about your teammates, and treat others with professionalism and respect so that you develop cohesion as a group. You may not love the people you work with, but you have to cooperate with one another in order to build a sense of collective faith in your ability to win.

All this leads me to the first key to managing team players, setbacks, and success: *Know your team players.* If you're a team player, this means knowing yourself and your teammates as you work to get the most out of your talents. (Throughout this book, I will use "team player" to mean anyone who works for an organization, whether it's sports or business.) If you're a manager, this means knowing the men and/or women you are trying to motivate in order to maximize their native abilities.

This chapter offers guidelines for knowing your team players—and yourself. It's a simple but profound rule—truly the first order of business for managers and workers alike. I offer my guidelines in these four sections:

1. Look into Their Eyes: Know Your Team Players
2. One-on-One: Make Time for Team Players
3. The Right Situation: Enable Players to Succeed
4. Look to Yourself: Know Your Skills, Limits, and Potential

We can never win unless we succeed in realizing our skills, and we can never realize our skills unless we know ourselves and the people we work with. Through my years of experience in baseball, I've embraced the idea that self-knowledge and knowledge of others is the launchpad for success and its by-product, winning.

Look into Their Eyes: Know Your Team Players

It's been said of me that as Yankee manager I have been able to bring many distinct personalities together into a cohesive unit. If I've succeeded in doing so, the key has been knowing my team players. By *know,* I mean several things: I know their skills. I know their potential. To some extent, I know their personalities. I try to know their needs as players and as people.

All these dimensions are significant. Some managers believe they only need to know their players' abilities so they can find the right slot for them in the field of play. That's essential, but I don't think it's enough. You have to take the pulse of your players, so you know who needs in-depth personal attention and who doesn't, who needs coaching and who doesn't, who needs a private dialogue with you and who doesn't, who you can count on in tough spots and who you can't. To develop this level of knowledge about your team players, you need some insight into their personal and emotional qualities. I'm not saying that managers should be psychics or psychotherapists. Nor do you have to be friends with your players, though friendships often grow out of the collective pursuit of a common goal. But you must be able to sense where your players are coming from—who they are and what kind of managerial attention will bring out the best in them.

A good example is Paul O'Neill, my right fielder since I came to the Yankees in 1996. Paul is the ultimate high-strung perfectionist. When he's not hitting well, he goes into an angry funk, often slamming his bat or his helmet after a tough at-bat. Even when he *is* hitting well, he may grimace or mouth private thoughts following a single unproductive turn at the plate. We know to leave Paul alone when he paces the dugout muttering to himself. On the broadcast for opening day of 1999, baseball commentator Tim McCarver said that for Paul O'Neill, "Every at-bat is Armageddon."

Now for some ballplayers, this kind of behavior is a worrisome sign. Many guys in prolonged slumps become frayed at the edges, and their anger at themselves festers until they lose all rhythm and poise at the plate. That rarely happens to Paul. Because I know him, I understand that Paul's frayed edges are different from those of other players. His high-strung behaviors are habits, not signs of serious trouble. Paul won't stay cold for long; he'll recover his timing, and his swing, often in a clutch situation. He'll usually work his way out of a slump without help from anyone, though he may sometimes make a batting adjustment. (During 1999 spring training, Paul was slumping when he received a phone call from Ted Williams, arguably the greatest pure hitter in the history of the game. Williams is a big fan of O'Neill, and he called with a minor but apparently useful bit of hitting advice.)

On one occasion, though, Paul had an emotional reaction to an event that was different from his usual flashes of anger at himself. It occurred at a pivotal point in the 1996 World Series, a moment where every decision I made seemed to have a life-or-death element. We'd been soundly beaten by the formidable Atlanta Braves in our first two games in Yankee Stadium, and were pronounced dead in the water by most of the sports media. But we came back to tie the series by winning two pressure-packed games at Fulton County Stadium in Atlanta, including an unforgettable comeback win in Game Four. As we approached Game Five, I had to decide who to play in several key positions. We'd be facing the Braves's exceptional right-handed pitcher, John Smoltz, so logic dictated that I play left-handed hitters Wade Boggs at third base, Tino Martinez at first, and Paul O'Neill in right field. I chose Charlie Hayes over Boggs, because Hayes had been getting big hits and he had a good record against Smoltz. Tino had been struggling at the plate, and in his place I had successfully used Cecil Fielder, who'd been getting clutch hits throughout the postseason. There was no compelling reason to switch back now. Paul had been bothered for weeks by a pulled leg muscle, and had not looked good at the plate. So I decided to play our veteran outfielder Tim Raines, as I had in our previous two wins, despite the fact that Raines hadn't been hitting much, either.

When I make such key decisions, I don't like to simply post the lineup without speaking first to my players who usually play every day (see chapter 3, Straight Communication: The Key to Trust). They deserve a face-to-face explanation. So I called each of them—Boggs, Martinez, and O'Neill—into my office, one by one. Boggs took the news reasonably well, but Martinez was obviously angry. Though he was our most productive hitter during the 1996 regular season, Tino lost his swing in the postseason, and when I told him I was going with Fielder he stalked out of my office, barely uttering a word.

O'Neill was next. I explained why I was playing Raines instead. He wasn't mad, like Tino. He was clearly hurt. He left my office, head down and shoulders slumped. Paul is such a fiery competitor that I was disturbed by his look of resignation.

A few minutes later, my bench coach, Don "Zim" Zimmer entered my office. "Paulie's down," he said. As I talked to Zimmer about the decision, it dawned on me that not playing Paul might affect his confidence for the remainder of the series, and I knew I might need him. Zimmer reminded me that Paul had played hurt most of the year, and hadn't been at the top of his game, yet he still gave the team everything he had. Raines was not batting well, either, so it had not been a clear-cut decision in which I owed it to the *team* to play Raines. I now felt I owed it to Paul to put him in the lineup. I said to Zim, "Let's play O'Neill."

Zimmer sent for O'Neill. When he walked into my office, I said, "You're playing." He was surprised but pleased. "That's what managers are allowed to do," I said. "Change their minds."

I never regretted changing my mind, even though Paul did not get a hit in Game Five. It was a heart-stopping pitchers' duel between Smoltz and our left-hander, Andy Pettitte. The score remained 1–0 through the bottom of the ninth, when Pettitte gave up a double to Chipper Jones, who moved to third on a grounder by Fred McGriff. I immediately brought in our closer, John Wetteland, who'd had a stellar year. Big John got Javier Lopez to ground out to Charlie Hayes, and Jones was held at third. We were one out away from taking an improbable lead in the World Series.

I had Wetteland intentionally walk Ryan Klesko, but after he did, Bobby Cox surprised me by sending Luis Polonia to pinch-hit instead of Terry Pendleton. Wetteland kept challenging Polonia with fastballs, who kept fouling them back, prolonging the agony. (Jose Cardenal, my first-base coach, noticed that Polonia was fouling balls to the left, so he moved Paul O'Neill toward center field.) Normally, John might have thrown a curveball into the mix, but he may have been fearful of a pitch in the dirt that could turn into a passed ball, allowing Jones to score the tying run. Finally, as Polonia saw another fastball coming, he knocked a fly ball to deep right-center field. The ball was hit out toward the warning track, but it looked playable, and I thought, There's the final out.

O'Neill ran toward the ball, but he appeared to step into a rough spot in the right-field grass, losing his balance for a moment. I remember thinking, either Paulie catches the ball and we go ahead in the series three games to two, or both runners score, we lose 2–1, and the Braves take a three-games-to-two lead. He was straining to run full speed on his bad leg, and as he reached the edge of the warning track, he made one last long stride with his arm fully outstretched. The ball landed in the brim of Paul's glove. We had secured the victory that brought us one win away from a world championship.

When I looked back on my change of mind, I felt as though I had been rewarded for trusting my instincts about playing Paul. He also contributed a key hit in Game Six at Yankee Stadium, a solid double to start a rally in the third inning. He scored the first run in what would be a 3–2 victory and a world championship for the 1996 Yankees.

Paul's reaction that day in my office was a signal that benching him could have had a serious downside—both for him and our club. The decision was based on an intangible: my read of his face and body language. But that, too, was based on knowing him as a unique individual. (We all recognize that different people's body language may mean different things: One friend's shrug could signal hurt while another's could mean disinterest.) That's why I tell managers in any field of endeavor, at any level in the organizational hierarchy, to know their team players. Don't dismiss this part of your job as secondary. In my view, it's primary—the foundation of your efforts to build teamwork and make right decisions.

Who can handle a tough middle-inning relief assignment? Who can deal with the pressure of pinch-hitting with two outs and the winning run on base in a postseason game? Who can you count on as a defensive replacement in the ninth, not only because he's a solid fielder but because you know he'll stay calm enough to make correct decisions? How can you help players to accept a backup role? If you don't know your team players, you won't have critical information at hand. It's a principle that holds in every business.

I recently spoke with Ken Venturi, the U.S. Open winner and golf analyst for CBS, about assessing people and their ability to handle pressure. "Always look in their eyes," said Venturi. "You'll see who they are, and what's special about them." Venturi was right, and it's something I've been doing for a long time. Some players can't look back at you, which tells you a lot about them. Not that they're bad players or lousy people who'll never come through in the clutch. Rather, they may be uncertain about themselves, and you need to take that into account. Such players often need more attention, and if you support them their confidence may blossom.

Looking in someone's eyes helps you figure out whether you can count on them in a crisis situation. In baseball, the classic example is the manager's trip to the mound to determine whether to replace a pitcher in a do-or-die situation. When you ask the general litmus question, "How are you feeling?" or the more specific ones, "How is your arm strength?" "How's the breaking ball?" or "Can you get the next batter?" you need an honest answer. If he can't look you in the eye when he says, "Fine," you can't be certain he's telling the truth.

But it's not just a player's truthfulness you can judge by looking in their eyes. Sometimes, you can see more, something about their character or their conviction. As Venturi said, you can see somebody special, and you need to know what's special about every one of your players in order to bring your team together to achieve a cherished goal.

One-on-One: Make Time for Team Players

What's involved in knowing team players? To know their abilities, you get reports from scouts and coaches, and closely observe them in practice and games. To know them as individuals, you need to look them in the eye. And you absolutely must make time for them. Sounds like a simple rule, but too many managers in too many walks of life only pay lip service to it.

Firstly, making time for team players enables you to appreciate them as individuals, which can definitely help you to get the most of their abilities. Secondly, it gives you opportunities to (1) let players know what you expect of them; (2) bolster their confidence; (3) answer their questions; and (4) offer support.

As I'll explain in chapter 3, I'm not big on team meetings—I prefer one-on-one sessions. I will hold hundreds of private discussions over the course of a single season, and these efforts are the basis of my motivational strategy. They may occur in my office, in the clubhouse by their lockers, on the field during practice, or on an airplane. It doesn't matter where the meeting occurs or how long it lasts. What matters is the quality of the exchange.

Private chats with your players should not feel like an obligatory routine. I suggest that you initiate them only "as needed," and only in circumstances where the door is open, so to speak. But when you do, use them for the reasons above—to better know your team players, and to use your communication skills to motivate them. Managers can use one-on-one meetings almost the way doctors use office visits —for both diagnosis and treatment.

One player who has benefited from private meetings is our second baseman, Chuck Knoblauch. Chuck is a hard worker who sets such lofty standards for himself that he occasionally tries too hard and stiffens in the field or at the plate. He was traded from the Minnesota Twins during the off-season, and when he joined our team in 1998 he was greeted with high expectations. We badly needed a reliable second baseman who could make a significant contribution on offense, and Chuck filled the bill. But it can be tough to come from such a small-market team to New York, with our intense media scrutiny and fans who never miss a trick. The pressure to make an impact right away, coupled with his own tendency to be hard on himself, led to some tough times for Chuck in his first season as a Yankee.

By the All-Star break, Knoblauch, a career .300 hitter, was batting only .258, and his fielding had become erratic, including a tendency to make wild throws to first on routine ground balls. Two games after the All-Star break, we had just beaten Tampa Bay when Chuck poked his head in my office and asked if we could meet the next afternoon. I said, "Why don't you come in right now?" I asked the crowd in my office to leave the room, and we spoke privately for half an hour.

We talked about what it meant to get acclimated to New York, what he expected of himself, and what we expected of him. I let Chuck know that I thought he was being tougher on himself than anyone else. I tried to allay his fears of any excessive expectations on our part. "My only expectation is that you play the way you play," I said. "The best way to achieve that is to be relaxed." While relaxing is often the key to optimal performance, it's never enough to tell someone to "just relax." Managers must create conditions in which team players can relax, and the best way is to offer ongoing guidance and reassurance. You don't have to hold their hands, you just have to make yourself available and be supportive.

Toward that end, I told Chuck about my time as a player that most closely mirrored his present circumstance. Before the 1969 season, I was traded from the Atlanta Braves to the Cardinals for Orlando Cepeda, a hugely popular and successful player in St. Louis. I put tremendous pressure on myself, wishing to impress everyone in the club (which included several superstars, such as Lou Brock, Curt Flood, Bob Gibson, and Steve Carlton), and live up to the high hopes fostered by the trade. I learned from that experience that trying to wow everyone while making impossible demands of yourself is a lethal combination—it only makes you tighten up more. You don't realize that this mind-set is totally counterproductive until much later, with the luxury of hindsight.

My conversation with Chuck helped us to know each other better, and I thought it set him at ease. His comfort level improved, and it showed in his play: He was more consistent in the field and more aggressive at the plate. During the next week, he hit home runs in three consecutive games. In the following two weeks, Chuck batted in 15 runs, slammed 6 homers, and made several sparkling plays at second base. He developed a softer game—one of grace and fluidity—rather than a clenched-jaw game. While he cooled off in the dog days of summer, he ended with respectable statistics, and he flourished in the World Series with a .375 batting average.

Key #1: Know Your Team Players

Here's my motto: *Every employee must feel useful.* In order to build teamwork, you must acknowledge each individual's worth, letting him know that his role, no matter how seemingly minor, is a vital cog in the team's efforts. When you grant your stars, your role-players, and everyone in between the same level of attention, you lay the groundwork for an unselfish team spirit, one where everyone belongs. I'm most proud of how the 1998 Yankees exemplified that team spirit; they left their egos behind and got the job done.

It's one thing to espouse the view that every team player must feel useful, but it's another to put it into practice. The only way is through the "make time" doctrine. Making time for team players is no panacea for their problems, but it's a fundamental rule of sound managing. It creates the space in which you can get to know them; let them know you; solidify trust; and resolve unspoken issues. Your one-on-one dialogues with team players are motivational building blocks—the basis for the creation of teamwork.

In the corporate world, with its increasing reliance on speedy high-tech solutions to every problem and the escalating demands of fierce (often global) competition, team players are under extreme pressure to work harder, longer, and more productively. (I always say that pressure is a given; deal with it rather than pretend it's not there.) These burdens can cause tension, burnout, and loss of creativity—something like the tightness ballplayers experience when they try too hard. Given the pressures on managers not only to supervise a work force but please higher-ups while answering countless questions and phone calls, it's not hard to understand why the "make time" doctrine is difficult to sustain. But good managers can help team players thrive under the toughest conditions by carving out time to communicate, reinforcing their importance to the team and its goals.

When you make time for employees, the *quality* of that time is also crucial. Managers must cultivate the ability to listen and sense what their team players are thinking and feeling. In his fine book, *Working with Emotional Intelligence,* Daniel Goleman makes this point forcefully, and I agree with him. One skill of emotional intelligence in the world of work is "understanding others." According to Goleman, people with this competence: (1) are attentive to emotional cues and listen well; (2) show sensitivity and understand others' perspectives; and (3) help out based on understanding other people's needs and feelings. On an instinctual basis, I've tried to follow these principles, and I can tell you that they work.

The Right Situation: Enable Players to Succeed

To get the most from the people you manage, you must put them in the right spot at the right time. I'm reminded of those TV lawyers who ask, "Did the suspect have the means, the motive, and the opportunity to commit this crime?" I want to make sure that my players have the means, the motive, and the opportunity to be winners. Opportunity is pivotal, and that means putting them in the right spot—giving them a chance to make the most of their talents.

Of course, every team has players who are totally secure in their positions—ace starting pitchers, star position players, reliable relief pitchers. I don't have to figure out what to do with our dazzling shortstop, Derek Jeter. Players like Derek establish themselves before you come on as manager, or they quickly establish themselves once you're on board. But there are many players—those platooned at a particular position, middle relievers, utility infielders, and pinch hitters—who do best in some situations and not in others. It's your job as manager to put them in situations in which they can succeed, and if you make sound decisions you give them the best chance to shine—and to help your team win. These "role-players" can be as important as your "stars," so this is crucial.

The "right spot" doctrine can be applied to any work environment—managers get the most from their talent by finding the best opportunities for each person and making sure everyone understands their importance to the organization. Likewise, employees succeed when they embrace their roles with professionalism, knowing that their contribution is vital for a winning team. But it's the manager's job to make sure that players are given optimal opportunities.

Everyone knows what author Tom Wolfe meant when he wrote his book about the astronauts of the 1960s and called it *The Right Stuff*. In my view, you won't have the right stuff if you're not in the right spot.

One Yankee who's shown he has the right stuff is Ramiro Mendoza. This soft-spoken right-hander has performed well in every role I've asked him to fill. He has ping-ponged from starter to middle reliever without losing his cool. Prior to the 1998 season, and at several other times during his tenure with the Yankees, there was talk within the Yankee organization about trading Mendoza, but I always argued against it. In his ability to make spot starts and then move right back to the bullpen for middle relief, he is very valuable. Others have done it, but few have done it as well as Ramiro. He's not recognized by the media as a star—few fans outside New York know much about him—but he's one of our most valuable contributors.

During 1998 spring training, Mendoza quickly emerged as the top choice for our fifth starting pitcher after David Cone, Andy Pettitte, David Wells, and Hideki Irabu. After getting off to a slow start in the regular season, Ramiro won three consecutive starts and found his comfort zone. When he's pitching well, Mendoza works fast and has pinpoint control. But he could not control fate, in the form of a Cuban defector who, legend has it, journeyed to this country on a rickety twenty-foot sailboat. That defector was Cuba's star pitcher, Orlando (El Duque) Hernandez. After a bidding war, we signed Hernandez and he joined us in spring training. He wasn't ready to start at the beginning of the season, so there was no question about Ramiro's selection. But fate intervened again when David Cone was bitten by his mother's Jack Russell terrier right on the ring finger of his pitching hand. We needed a replacement, so on June 3, I gave Hernandez his first opportunity to start. He was so effective, allowing only one run and five hits in a 7–1 victory over the Devil Rays, that I felt we had to let him continue as a starter. After Cone returned, El Duque replaced Mendoza in the regular rotation.

When I told Ramiro that El Duque was going to be one of our starters, he was openly unhappy. I explained that I didn't expect him to be thrilled with the decision, only to accept it. (I'd be wary of a player who had no negative reaction to being benched or taken out of the starting rotation.)

But I emphasized that we selected him for the bullpen because he could perform better in relief than any of the other starters. Ramiro has the rare durability and flexibility to pitch well whenever he's called upon, for as many innings as we need him. He could do as much (or more) to help us win as a middle reliever, and I told him so.

Many pitchers would respond to this seeming demotion by letting themselves and their teammates down. While I know he was disappointed, Ramiro never allowed his emotions to interfere with his competitive drive; maybe he found a way to use them as fuel. (It would be hard to know, because he rarely shows his feelings.) His ERA as a starter was a decent 3.87; as a reliever, it was an outstanding 1.93. But Ramiro saved his best for the postseason, when he was a critical link in several victories on the road to our world championship.

Our greatest challenge in 1998 was the American League championship series against the Cleveland Indians, who had knocked us out of contention in the 1997 division playoffs. After winning the first game in the series, we lost two straight and had our backs against the wall for the first time in our record-breaking season. We fought back in Cleveland to win Games Four and Five, putting us up three games to two, and we returned to Yankee Stadium needing only one victory to get to the World Series. But Cleveland had the rattlesnake-like ability to strike at any time, and we'd been badly bitten in 1997 when they stole our chance to repeat our 1996 triumph. I wanted us to finish them off in Game Six, and we had David Cone on the mound, who had proven his ability to handle the thorniest postseason assignments.

Cone was cruising along with a shutout, staked to a 6–0 lead with the help of a third-inning, three-run blast by third baseman Scott Brosius. David had eight strikeouts and it looked like our American League championship would be a cakewalk. But he tired in the fifth, and the roof caved in. Three consecutive hits loaded the bases, and Cone walked David Justice to force home a run. He struck out Manny Ramirez, and the next batter was the dangerous Jim Thome. David tried to slip a slider under his hands, but the pitch hung over the middle of the plate. Thome hammered the ball into the upper deck in right field. His grand slam left us with a slim 6–5 lead, and a desperate need to stanch the bleeding.

I brought in Ramiro, who proceeded to shut down the Indians in the sixth, seventh, and eighth innings. I could not have asked for more, since I knew I could count on my phenomenal closer, Mariano Rivera, to finish the job in the ninth. During those three sparkling innings, Mendoza did not allow a single runner past first base. We got three insurance runs in the sixth, and went on to beat the Indians 9–5, enabling us to make our second trip to the World Series in my three-year tenure with the Yanks.

Had we not had Mendoza as a stabilizer, Jim Thome's rocket of a home run might have spelled an end to our glorious season. His fearless efforts under duress helped us to win, and it was a perfect example of how our team players instantly took up the slack when one of us was struggling. It happened all year long. When the top batters in our order were slumping, the bottom third of the order was hot. When shortstop Derek Jeter was injured, utility infielder Luis Sojo got the job done. When Darryl Strawberry was diagnosed with colon cancer at the end of the year, Chili Davis ably filled his shoes as designated hitter. During the clubhouse champagne celebration after we beat the Indians, David Cone turned to Mendoza and said, "Thanks for picking me up."

Ramiro picked us up many times in 1998, including his three postseason relief appearances, during which his ERA was a skimpy 1.69. He was the winning pitcher in Game Three of the World Series against the San Diego Padres, based on his brief but significant contribution to a tight, come-from-behind 5–4 victory.

Mendoza continues to thrive because he's been put in the right spot and made the most of it, time and again. In 1999, we came out of spring training expecting our starters to be the newly acquired Roger Clemens, David Cone, Orlando Hernandez, Andy Pettitte, and Hideki Irabu. But Irabu faltered badly as the regular season approached, and my bench coach, Don Zimmer, who took over as manager during my recovery from prostate surgery, had to replace him in the starting rotation. Who else but Mendoza? He began the season in typical fashion, winning three of his first five starts and posting a solid 3.03 ERA. In mid-May, though, it became apparent that our middle relievers were struggling; this cost us a number of early games. Roger Clemens had been injured, and when Irabu took Clemens's spot he pitched well enough to allow Zimmer to keep him in the rotation. Clemens returned after I was back in the dugout, so I was able to to put Ramiro back in the bullpen where he could shore up our middle relief.

Most players would become carsick, or even worse, heartsick, over so many lurching shifts. Not Ramiro. He didn't mope or complain, because he fully understood that his move back to long relief was a sign of respect for his ability. We so badly needed a stabilizing force in the bullpen, and he was the only man who could give us that. We let Mendoza know that going back to the bullpen was not a punishment. He understood that we valued him as a starter, and that he'd be back in the rotation at the drop of a hat if we needed him there.

Managers must find the right spot for team players, but players must make the best of the roles in which they've been cast. Mendoza does that, and so does our utility infielder Luis Sojo, our designated hitter Chili Davis, our middle relievers Jeff Nelson and Mike Stanton, and our platooning left fielders Shane Spencer, Ricky Ledee, and Chad Curtis, to name a few. They've all had their lapses, but over the long haul—and baseball, like life, is a long haul—they play their parts effectively.

As Yankee manager, I've been blessed to have so many remarkable role-players. In 1998, backup second baseman Homer Bush was a brilliant spark plug off the bench as a pinch runner—a guy who used his speed and aggressiveness on the base paths to give us a lift almost every time I put him in. From the time we acquired him in 1996, left-handed reliever Graeme Lloyd made the most of his assignment—to get out dangerous left-handed batters during late-inning jams. Often, I would call on him to get one batter and remove him immediately thereafter. Lloyd, who we traded to the Blue Jays in the Roger Clemens deal, was like the surgeon who does only one procedure, but does it so well that he's in tremendous demand. In fact, on the mound he often operates like a surgeon. During the 1996 postseason, Lloyd was so effective in so many critical situations that he repeatedly made me look like a genius. But he was the genius; I merely knew when to bring him in from the bullpen.

If the unprecedented success of the '98 Yankee team was a puzzle, the big picture was clear and whole and perfect because each piece was in its proper place. Each player made his contribution, in the right spot at the right time.

Again, managers must know their people in order to make sound decisions about the right spots. You must know their "skill sets," to borrow the corporate lingo. You must know their temperaments. You must know their strengths and vulnerabilities.

As an employee, you must (1) know your *own* skills, strengths, and weaknesses; (2) put *yourself* in positions to succeed by finding ways to demonstrate your talents; and (3) accept your assigned role by being professional, and by being willing to work diligently to fulfill your promise, even if you don't completely agree with your manager's decision.

Workers sometimes have trouble with point number three. When they feel they've been put in the wrong positions, they may complain, harbor resentment, and put in less-than-optimal effort.

In such cases, as a team player, it may help to communicate your concerns to the manager, if only to open up a dialogue. It never helps to let resentments fester; I've always favored getting conflicts and issues out on the table. By the same token, you should make your statement without the expectation that your manager will oblige your wishes. He may or may not, but the point should be to clear the air, not manipulate the manager into giving you what you want. You may even be right, but it's the supervisor's job to decide where you belong, and it's a waste of energy and emotion trying to fight such battles. (If you're in a position where your talents are always wasted or undermined, you generally have the option to leave and find another job. However, this is rarely easy. Mostly we must do our best to improve our working conditions before considering a difficult move.) Once you've had your say, there's a good chance your relationship with your manager will improve, even if the manager doesn't change his or her mind. I know that Ramiro Mendoza was displeased when I put him in the bullpen in '98, but we knew where we stood with each other, and he quickly flourished in his role.

You can flourish in your role as a team player, as long as you put your whole self into the tasks you've been given. Wait your turn; work with passion and conviction; and recognize how your special talents are valuable to the team and its larger goals. Speak up if you think you've been mistreated. In any well-managed organization, your efforts will be noticed, appreciated, and rewarded by supervisors and upper-level managers. If your fervent hope is that your role will expand in some way, there's a chance it will. I can tell you this: Managers not only appreciate the talent that goes into a job well done, they notice the ability to handle disappointments with patience and professionalism.

What matters most is the match between the team player and his or her role, and it's the manager's task to make sure it's the right fit. When managers and players both do their jobs, team players will get an opportunity to show that they've got the right stuff.

Look to Yourself: Knowing Your Skills, Limits, and Potential

Managers must know the people they manage, but as a team player you must know yourself, and by that I mean acknowledging your skills, your limits, and your potential.

Recognizing your own talents is crucial. Team players need a complete awareness of who they are and what they do well professionally. This requires a balanced view of your skills, limits, and potential. For instance, if you think you're a home run king like Mark McGwire of the Cards when you're really a good contact hitter like John Olerud of the Mets, you're in trouble. The successful ballplayer knows his strengths and skills, and he avoids fruitless attempts to be someone he isn't. Likewise, the successful team player in the business world knows his strengths and skills, and he sidesteps the temptation to move far outside the realm of his abilities. Imagine for a moment that a movie casting director lost his sanity and tried to cast Dustin Hoffman as James Bond and Sean Connery as Tootsie. These are both versatile actors, but they'd be making the worst blunder of their careers if they took the bait.

Part of knowing yourself as a team player, therefore, is accepting your limits. On occasion in 1998, our lead-off hitter Chuck Knoblauch got himself into trouble trying to belt home runs. He hit seventeen homers—a career high—but there were times when he'd swing for the fences and was less effective at the plate (though I hardly minded when he slammed a three-run shot to tie Game One of the World Series, setting the stage for a dramatic victory). Here's the key point: As our lead-off man, Chuck's job is to get on base, setting the table for the ever-dangerous Derek Jeter, the clutch-hitting Paul O'Neill, and the power-hitting heart of our order, Bernie Williams, Tino Martinez, and Chili Davis or Darryl Strawberry. For a lead-off hitter like Chuck, on-base percentage is a more important statistic than batting average. I have no problem if the count is in his favor and he swings away, but he would not serve himself or the team well if he consistently tried to hit balls out of the park. Chuck has come to recognize this, and he continues to make adjustments that improve his hitting. He's also shown more maturity in how he's handled the pressures of playing in New York, a sign that he knows himself better as a ballplayer and a person.

There's a baseball cliché that sums this up: *Stay within yourself.* Like many clichés, this one happens to be true, but it also contains deeper wisdom that you can apply beyond baseball. You've probably heard baseball commentators suggest that a batter at the plate or pitcher on the mound must stay within himself. It means that he should not try to do more than is possible; that he know what pitches he can hit or throw and does not move outside his range of ability; that he remains patient, focused, and grounded in the moment.

Workers and players in all fields can benefit by taking the maxim "stay within yourself" to heart. *Recognizing our limits can also be a way to recognize our strengths.* When we totally ignore our limitations, we end up forgetting our strengths—trying to do more than we can, trying to be someone we're not—and we lose our instincts, our spontaneity, and our confidence.

Now here is a paradox. Once we know our true talents, acknowledging strengths and limits, we can sometimes exceed expectations for what we can accomplish. Having recognized our limits, we can actually realize our limitless potential. The exceptions are stars who do everything well, who appear to have few limits on their ability (one such player is Ken Griffey Jr., a spectacular fielder, RBI man, and power hitter). But most high achievers have a specialty. Once they recognize their specialty, work hard to perfect it, and become mature and focused in their efforts, they can blow the lid off all expectations. A conspicuous example is Mark McGwire, who continued to evolve as a power hitter through the 1990s until he finally shattered Roger Maris's single-season record of 61 home runs with his astonishing 70 round-trippers.

Here's an explosive equation: Add knowledge of your own strengths to a maximum effort to improve, and you have a formula for success. I have seen this formula work with many of the Yankees I've managed, but one particularly comes to mind. Derek Jeter knows his abilities at shortstop, and he's a supremely self-assured batter who is patient and relaxed at the plate. He has power, but he doesn't try to blast home runs unless he gets the kind of pitch he can handle. One of his strengths is going with the pitch, slapping balls on the outside corner of the plate for opposite-field base hits. (Going with the pitch is an example of working with what you're given.) He is totally unflappable, thriving on pressure the way kids in a schoolyard game thrive on a dare.

Jeter surpasses expectations, partly because he's not afraid to make a mistake, to embarrass himself. He'll often grab a ground ball deep in the hole between short and third, twist his body in midair, and while still airborne, whip a perfect throw to first base that beats the runner in a photo finish.

I've seen him blow that play, but he usually succeeds. Some batters think it's embarrassing to get jammed by inside pitches, but not Jeter. When he gets jammed, it doesn't bother him one bit.

I remember that in grade school I'd be afraid to raise my hand for fear that other kids or the teacher would think my question was dumb. I always had great admiration for the kids who asked the dumb questions, because they were the questions I wanted to ask. But my career in baseball has taught me that you accomplish less when you expend all your energy trying to sidestep mistakes. A player like Derek Jeter will be more successful because he's not afraid to make a mistake. You can be unafraid to stumble without being reckless or careless. If you work diligently at the fundamentals of your sport, trade, or business, and you continually strive for excellence, you can take risks and you'll often be rewarded. Jeter is being rewarded, and while it's still early in his career, he has the look of a ballplayer who may get the ultimate reward—a place in the Hall of Fame.

My catcher Joe Girardi once paid me a high compliment when he said of me: "He gets the most out of every one of his players." As manager, I'm only responsible for part of that equation. I know my players, make time for them, and try to put them in positions to succeed. The rest is up to them.

To get the most out of yourself, you must know yourself—your strengths, your limits, your potential. Stay within yourself, but recognize that within those bounds there is no telling what you can accomplish. Don't be reckless in your pursuit of individual and team goals, but don't be afraid to make mistakes, either. Accept these paradoxes—you can acknowledge your limits and yet exceed all expectations; you can be disciplined and careful in your work habits, but fearless as you strive to realize your highest potential. Self-knowledge plus maximum effort is a valid formula for success.

Torre's Winning Ways
Key #1: Know Your Team Players

- **Know Your Team Players**
  - Their professional skills and abilities.
  - Their character and personal qualities.
  - Their reliability under pressure.

- **Make Time for Team Players**
  - Carve out time for one-on-one dialogue.
  - Help each individual understand their importance to the team.
  - Use dialogue to:
    1. Let employees know what you expect of them.
    2. Bolster their confidence.
    3. Answer questions and respond to concerns.
    4. Offer support.

- **Enable Players to Succeed**
  - Give team players means, motive, and opportunity to succeed.
  - Find the role that best matches each team player's skills.
  - Give him or her ample opportunity to fulfill that role.

- Reinforce the importance of his or her contribution, no matter how seemingly minor.
- Remember that putting a team player in the right spot brings out the right stuff.

- **Know Your Limits, Skills, and Potential**
  - Recognize your own talents and skill sets.
  - Stay within yourself—know your limits—but realize that within those bounds your potential is limitless.
  - Remember that knowledge of your own strengths combined with maximum effort to improve, yields a formula for success.

CHAPTER 2 **Key #2:**

Fairness, Respect, and Trust: Torre's Triple Play

Fairness, respect, and trust are the three prime ingredients in any recipe for teamwork. Offer fairness, respect, and trust to your team players, and they will respond in kind. Not only will your employees grant you the same decency you grant them, they will begin to demonstrate these values with one another, which only cements the spirit of togetherness and commitment that fuels great teams.

I know that this approach is effective, because I've seen it work with the Yankees. I follow six clear-cut rules that represent the foundations of fairness, respect, and trust, rules that I believe have contributed to our two world championships:

1. I treat team players with honesty and trust, and ask for the same in return.
2. I make an unstated agreement with each team player: "Give me effort and I'll never second-guess you. I'll always defend you."

3. I apply team rules evenhandedly to all team members.

4. I never air grievances to others, including the media, before I privately air my grievance with a player.

5. I never humiliate or embarrass a team player in front of others.

6. I don't play favorites. I offer no special favors to high-salaried stars or players I like, nor do I make a show of personal preferences.

These six rules are not universally embraced by managers in sports or business. Some managers use fear, favoritism, manipulation, or public humiliation to light sparks under their employees. I won't judge anyone else's managerial style, and in some instances these tactics appear to work. But they don't suit my personality, and I wasn't comfortable when they were applied to me by managers during my years as a player. I've always found that a managerial style rooted in the "triple play" of fairness, respect, and trust promotes teamwork and a winning attitude. This approach makes it enjoyable to be part of a team, and it makes membership in the group a source of pride for each team player.

My philosophy has sometimes led baseball critics or media to label me a "player's manager," a tag that usually carries a negative connotation. When I managed the Mets, the general manager, Frank Cashen, thought I was too "soft" as a manager. I'd been fired three times—from the Mets, Braves, and Cardinals—and I was dogged afterward by criticisms. There were times when I second-guessed my own approach, wondering if I should be a tougher disciplinarian. While I struggled with this question, my gut told me that my managerial approach was best for *me*. It was an outgrowth of my character and beliefs, and if I tried to substantially alter how I managed I would not be true to myself, and my players would see through me.

Before I began as Yankee manager, I picked up Bill Parcells's book, *Finding a Way to Win*. I came across one comment that stayed with me: If you believe in something, stick with it. It was a simple piece of wisdom but it struck the right chord at that pivotal moment. I needed to remind myself, after many rough times as a manager over nearly two decades, and six years as a broadcaster, that I should stick to my guns and manage as I saw fit.

It was ironic that this affirming piece of advice should come from Parcells, head coach of the New York Jets, a man I know and respect. His style is almost diametrically opposed to mine, but works spectacularly well for him and his players. He is a different personality in an entirely different sport with a unique set of players and challenges. While I believe that managers and employees must change and mature, we all have a core set of beliefs that guide how we conduct ourselves as professionals, and we should honor them.

Some managers may be too lax or friendly with players in ways that don't serve the team. But in baseball, many skippers tagged "players' managers" are highly effective and don't deserve all that carping. A successful players' manager may be friendly, but he doesn't play favorites. One who comes to mind is Davey Johnson, a laid-back guy who has never been a traditional disciplinarian, but who's been a winning manager every place he's gone. (The fact that Davey won the world championship with the Mets and has continued to be a winner since, hasn't stopped the criticism.) A players' manager is considered OK when he wins, but "too soft" when he loses.

My gut instinct has always been that in the right circumstances, my approach—however you label it—would not only work, it would enable a group of hungry team players to scale the heights of baseball success. Fortunately, in 1996, George Steinbrenner gave me a chance to do just that.

My core philosophy is this: If I treat players as responsible adults, and I apply a modest set of rules equally and fairly, I should not have to dictate their every move. It helps to have a grown-up group like the Yankees, who've obviously blossomed under this approach. But you can apply the same philosophy with players who don't appear to be as motivated or mature, and they often rise to the standard you have set.

When they joined the Yankees, the two ex-Mets Dwight Gooden and Darryl Strawberry were given rough treatment by some in the media who asked: How could these two fallen stars, with their personal and professional troubles, past substance abuse, and inability to fulfill their early promise, succeed with any team, let alone the team under the highest power microscope of any in sports? In the years I have managed them, both men have not only been professional, likable, and cooperative, they've made major contributions to world championship seasons. I don't take credit for their accomplishments with the Yankees, but I do believe that when I crossed paths with Dwight and Darryl, they were receptive to being treated as responsible adults. I know it helped that I gave each one a clean slate, judging and treating them based on their current behavior and performance rather than past reputations. Both players thrived in a group where fairness, respect, and trust were the governing principles.

I see evidence of this philosophy taking hold in the corporate world—particularly in the high-tech sector—where executives and managers are putting the highest premium on hard work and creativity, while giving up the need for strict control over every facet of their employees' work lives. Many executives are coming to recognize that team players can be more highly motivated in an atmosphere of mutual respect and collective commitment rather than one of dictatorial control, rigid performance standards, and fear-based supervision.

But does this philosophy really work in the corporate world? There's solid evidence that it does. In his book, *Working with Emotional Intelligence,* Daniel Goleman mentions a survey of fifty-eight top managers, all vice presidents or higher at companies with annual sales of five billion dollars or more. The managers were asked about their experiences with on-the-job coaching. What was the key to successful coaching? "Trust was crucial," writes Goleman in his summary of the findings. "When there was little trust in the coach, advice went unheeded . . . Coaches who showed respect, trustworthiness, and empathy were the best."

I offer my guidelines to "Torre's triple play" in these three sections:

1. Apply Fairness: All Players Are Created Equal
2. Respect: Give It to Get It
3. Trust: The Foundation of Teamwork

As you read through these guidelines, recognize that the success I've had applying them in baseball is possible in any realm of business and social organization, including family relations. I strongly believe that fairness, respect, and trust should be the governing principles of every group endeavor. Whatever your field of dreams, this triple play can become a reality.

Apply Fairness: All Players Are Created Equal

In 1969, I was traded from the Braves to the St. Louis Cardinals, where I joined a tremendous bunch of baseball players. It was my ninth year in the big leagues, but in my six years with the Cards, I learned and matured more than at any other time as a ballplayer. This was partly due to the influence of my teammates, including catcher Tim McCarver, now a renowned baseball analyst for the FOX network and the New York Yankees; Hall of Fame pitcher Bob Gibson; and shortstop Dal Maxvill. (The four of us formed what we called "the Dinner Club": we met regularly to eat gourmet food, drink fine wines, and talk endlessly about the finer points of baseball strategy.) When I first arrived, the Cards had just won two pennants; they were a cool, collected, seasoned group of men who taught me a great deal about class and professionalism.

But the tone was set from the top, as it so often is. The

manager, Red Schoendienst, was fair and evenhanded in his managerial style. Unlike other managers in my past, he didn't nickel and dime us to death. By that I mean he never imposed arbitrary rules just to aggravate players. He trusted us as professionals, treated us like professionals, and we acted like professionals. In our case, we were a motivated and mature group to begin with. But I have no doubt that we were more cohesive and responsible because of the way we were treated by Schoendienst. When I became Yankee manager, I was reminded of those Cardinal teams. With the Yankees, I've been able to manage with the confidence that my team players would heed the basic rules, understand my moves, and accept my judgments—even if they didn't always agree. Schoendienst was a good managerial model, one I have kept in mind throughout my career on the bench.

Times have changed radically since those days, what with free agency; multiyear, multimillion-dollar contracts; and lucrative endorsement deals. Too often, players' egos become just as inflated as their huge bank accounts. It's easy to understand, especially when many such players are still too young to be expected to handle all that money and media scrutiny with maturity.

Think about it: If your everyday team players, from whom you need supreme effort, notice star players being treated as an elite who receive special privileges, it's bound to lessen their commitment. In time, this wears away at their team spirit because some players harbor resentment toward guys right next to them in the clubhouse.

The solution is simple, a virtual quick fix for organizational discontent: Be absolutely equitable in how you treat team players. Don't give anyone an extra edge because the media loves him, or he's just cut a big money deal with upper management. Unless managers maintain fairness and even-handedness with all their players, treating the high-priced talent no differently from the others, the money-and-ego factor can erode teamwork. (This applies in the business world as well, where executives on the same level of the hierarchy are sometimes treated better than others because of their pay scale rather than their performance.) In baseball, there are three areas in which I make certain to treat players fairly and equally: (1) decisions about playing time; (2) my requirement that everyone be prepared; and (3) adherence to team rules, such as showing up on time and travelling together on the team bus.

As with many team sports, the issue of playing time is the most emotionally charged. I must play the guys who I think give me the best chance each day. A benched player may have bruised feelings, but normal disappointment turns to something worse when he feels he's been bypassed because the other guy makes more money or is a manager's favorite. Every team player must believe that he'll get a fair shot if he's earned it based on performance. In the corporate world, the rough equivalent is deciding who gets the big account or the prized promotion. If people are picked for reasons other than merit, team morale is going to suffer.

Baseball and business are quite alike in this regard. Highly paid stars or well-liked players must accept that they'll sit if they are not getting the job done, or if they're not the right player on a given night against a given team. In the 1996 World Series, I sat the slumping Tino Martinez in favor of Cecil Fielder at first base, even though Tino was my best hitter during the regular season. It was difficult to break the news, and Tino was certainly upset. But I believe he understood the basis for my decision—that we had a better chance to win with Cecil that day. He also knew that my action didn't mean I'd lost trust in him over the long term. Tino knows how highly I regard him as a person and a player. By the same token, I was being fair to Fielder, who was contributing clutch hits and deserved to play against the Braves in Atlanta, where I did not have the option of playing him as a designated hitter. Ultimately, I was being fair to the team. It would be an injustice to all twenty-five players if I didn't do everything I thought was right to win.

I believe in the old maxim: "Go with who got you there." I am also intensely loyal—some would say to a fault—to players who've consistently given me 100 percent effort. Over a long regular season, it's easier to give players and pitchers opportunities to gradually work their way out of dry spells. But in the postseason, you can't operate that way. I still try to "go with who got me there," but in critical situations I must be flexible enough to make lineup changes that give us the best chance to win that day.

In the 1998 postseason, I was forced to do a great deal of juggling in left field. We lost Darryl Strawberry, who'd had a terrific year despite a gimpy leg, when in late September he was stricken with suspicious abdominal pains. (On the day before our third game in the division series against the Texas Rangers, we learned that Darryl had been diagnosed with colon cancer. Needless to say, we were shocked and saddened.) Both of our other left fielders, Chad Curtis and the veteran Tim Raines, were not hitting with any consistency. I needed another option.

Enter Shane Spencer. In the final weeks of September, around the time that we lost Darryl, we brought up this fair-haired kid with a boyish face, a sturdy hitter who'd shown flashes of power potential during his eight years in the minors. (He started out as a twenty-eighth-round draft pick in 1990.) We brought him up from our Triple A Columbus team several times during 1998, but nothing prepared us for his performance during the month of September. In a mere 38 at-bats, he smacked 8 home runs and knocked in 21 runs, while batting .421. But his most remarkable feat was belting three grand slams in a span of ten days. It had taken my entire sixteen-year playing career to hit three grand slams! (For the record, Spencer's grand slams came in a mere 67 at-bats; mine came in 7,874 at-bats.) He reminded me of the fictional baseball legends Roy Hobbs in *The Natural* and Joe Hardy in the play *Damn Yankees*. I guess that such feats could only be dreamed up in stories.

We were all dazzled by Spencer's performance, but when I had to decide who to play during the postseason, I considered many factors. I had to weigh Spencer's phenomenal hitting streak against the experience and fielding prowess of Chad Curtis, and the reliability of a seasoned veteran like Tim Raines. I chose to play Curtis in the first game of our division series against Texas, since he had good numbers against pitcher Todd Stottlemyre, and then insert Spencer for the second and third games of the series. Just two months earlier, Curtis had signed a three-year, multimillion-dollar contract. If I'd been thinking about Curtis in these terms, I might not have given Spencer an opportunity to take his place in September, nor would I have put him in the lineup against Texas, and later Cleveland in the postseason. But like a gambler on a hot streak, I had to keep rolling with Spencer, who'd been lighting up the sky with home runs. I explained the move to Curtis, a steadfast team player who understood my rationale.

Curtis contributed a key hit and scored one of our runs in a 2–0 victory, behind the brilliant pitching of David Wells. But I stuck with my plan to play Spencer in the second game, and he didn't disappoint. In his very first postseason at-bat, Shane smacked a 2–2 pitch over the left-field fence, right into Monument Park where the Yankees legends are memorialized. Later, he scored a run on Scott Brosius's three-run blast, in a game we won 3–0.

The next game in Texas was an intense pitching duel between David Cone and Aaron Sele, who both put goose eggs on the scoreboard through five innings. But in the top of the sixth, Paul O'Neill lined a home run into our bullpen. Later in that inning, with two outs and two men on base, Spencer came to bat. Sele had been throwing a lot of curveballs, and Shane was mad at himself because he'd popped one up in an earlier at-bat. He expected more curves, and when the first pitch was a hanging breaking ball, he was ready for it. Shane blasted the ball into the left-field seats, a three-run shot that gave us a 4–0 lead. That would remain the score, after a three-hour and sixteen-minute rain delay. We had won the division series three games to none, and would move on to face Cleveland for the American League championship.

I continued to juggle left fielders throughout the 1998 postseason, and when Shane cooled off in the Cleveland series I turned to another rookie, Ricky Ledee, who we called up from the minors after Darryl became sick. Like Shane, Ricky also made stellar contributions in the postseason, this time in the World Series against San Diego. Our situation in left field illustrates the fairness doctrine I have been preaching and practicing for years. I owe it to the team to play the individual I think gives us the best chance to win that particular game. A hot streak is only one factor I bear in mind. I must also consider playoff experience, fielding ability, clutch-hitting prowess, trustworthiness, and grace under pressure. I must not factor in salary, star status, friendship, or the preferences of anyone in the front office.

All of these team players—Raines, Curtis, Spencer, and Ledee—accepted my decisions professionally. I know that each was disappointed when they were not in the lineup, but they weren't dejected. This is exactly the kind of response I would expect—and wish for. I'm suspicious of players who don't seem to mind warming the bench. I want team players with so much competitive fire that they are dying to be on the field every day. But I also don't want players to become dispirited. When I make these decisions with absolute fairness, they know that they'll get a chance. As long as they give their utmost effort, I will provide them with opportunities to produce.

The kind of decisions I make about daily platooning strike me as comparable to ones that constantly arise in the business world. Who gets the plum assignment? Who's put in charge of the most lucrative accounts? Who gets to take the most exciting trips? Who gets the primo perks? If people feel they're not getting a fair shake, they are bound to feel less excited about coming to work.

Of course, not everyone is going to get the best assignments or promotions. That's where communication is key. As a manager, if you take the time to explain your reasoning to your people—if you remind them of your faith in their ability and your promise to find the right spots for them—they won't lose their motivation or commitment to the team.

In any business, workers up and down the hierarchy want nothing more than to be treated fairly, to feel that they aren't getting the short end of a manager's stick. My second baseman in 1996, Mariano Duncan, once was quoted as saying about me, "He doesn't play favorites. All twenty-five guys are his favorites." It was kind of him to say, and I believe that it's true. Managers who make it their business to keep personal preferences to themselves, to show regard for all employees, and to be scrupulously fair about opportunities, promotions, and perks, will be rewarded with a bunch of highly motivated team players.

Rules of Order: Use Flexibility

I don't have too many rules for the Yankees, but I expect everyone to follow them, and it's my job to enforce them equitably. I always say that you can't treat each player the same way because everyone is different, but when it comes to team rules, you must treat everyone the same. In other words, you may teach, motivate, and relate to each person differently, but you apply basic standards of conduct across the board.

For the Yankees, I've set forth what I believe is a set of reasonable rules. We have a written list of them, so players can't claim ignorance. The primary ones are: Show up on time; No excuses for lateness; Everyone should be ready to go in uniform at the designated time; No children in the clubhouse until after the game; Players must travel on the team bus unless cleared by me; Everyone must be out on the field for the National Anthem; Headphones are required for listening to music; and No excessive facial hair.

Then there are the unwritten rules: Run hard, play hard, and be prepared. In my book, whether you're making one hundred thousand dollars per year or ten million, you're required to run hard to first base.

The rule about being neatly groomed is one that George Steinbrenner has had in place for a long time. Years before I came to the team, George enforced it with the most popular Yankee in those days, Don Mattingly, who often had tufts of hair protruding from the back of his baseball cap. I've held on to the rule in deference to George, who didn't seem to mind when pitcher David "Boomer" Wells, ever the rebel, began to sport a scratchy goatee. George apparently felt that David was a unique personality who should be cut some slack, especially when he was winning. But I feel that if I have a rule I ought to uphold it with everyone, so I was always after David to shave his goatee. Not my favorite managerial task.

At first blush, the headphones rule may seem like nitpicking, but it's not. When you have a group as diverse as ours, you've got people passionately drawn to various types of music. David Wells was a heavy metal fanatic, and had we not required him to use headphones, we'd have had some pretty cranky players in our clubhouse, not to mention the manager who loves Sinatra. (Though I did make a concession by letting Boomer play his music aloud on days he was our starter.)

Every rule serves a purpose, and taken together, these rules reinforce professional behavior, common courtesy, concentration on baseball, and the smooth functioning of the group. During my first year, when we instituted the National Anthem rule, I wanted everyone out on the field stretching, ready to line up when the Anthem was sung. I knew it was working—that I'd established the right mood—when players started policing one another on this point. I wanted them to care about any rule designed to enhance our professionalism, our respect for each other and the game.

But I also try to be flexible. If you're far too rigid, players start to doubt the purpose of your rules, as if the code isn't designed to achieve team coherence and mutual respect, but rather to make life difficult for no particular reason. For instance, I expect players to travel with the club, but I'll make exceptions if a player comes to me with a specific request. If we have an off day and someone wants to meet us in the next city on a road trip, as long as he has a valid reason I'll usually allow it. In today's world, team players always have something going on in their lives—family that needs tending, a health problem, business matters that require attention. You've got to adapt your rules to the reality of people's lives and the culture we live in.

My motto is this: I give team players plenty of freedom and a trunkful of responsibility, and see how much they can handle. If you have a group of adults like the 1996–1998 Yankees, they rise to the occasion with great maturity. If you're not so lucky, you must make adjustments in your rules and how you enforce them, loosening or tightening as your instincts tell you is necessary. For the most part–whether you're managing in the world of sports, school, or business– when you give workers ample amounts of freedom *and* responsibility, including a clear set of guidelines for professional conduct, they usually meet or exceed your expectations.

Fairness Builds Togetherness

I often make the analogy between teams and families. It's been said before, and it may seem old-fashioned. But no matter how often the analogy is applied, I still see teams in sports and business where upper and middle managers don't pay attention to the needs of their team players and don't treat people with fairness. That tells me that they don't understand the ways in which teams are like families.

Teams are not really families, but there are many crucial similarities. Families thrive when members grant one another time; follow agreed-upon rules; treat one another with fairness, respect, and trust; and make togetherness a top priority. Sports and business teams are no different. It's that simple.

When managers follow this version of the family model, and workers do their part, the team begins to cultivate qualities–like caring and cooperation–that breed success. Players on teams that operate on this model will also experience a sense of joy in their daily work, and that's never a bad thing. (I'll return to this theme with Key #12, "The Game of Life: Sacrifice Is Not Just a Bunt.")

I'm particularly proud of how my Yankee teams—all of them, but especially the '98 group—have been a collection of diverse personalities from totally different ethnic and religious backgrounds, who've managed to get along and respect one another. With regard to the 1998 Yankees, I've never seen a team develop such strong bonds of love and cooperation, and I'm certain it helped them to achieve their goals. I don't take credit for their sense of togetherness, but I do think I helped lay the groundwork by treating them equitably.

Remember this: When as a manager you are rigorously fair, you diminish griping, backbiting, and hidden resentments—a kind of disease that saps team spirit. By the same token, you create a spirit of cooperation, mutual respect, and commitment to team goals.

Respect: Give It to Get It

I was a major league ballplayer for sixteen years, and some of my managers were old-school characters who used fear and threats to try to motivate. You can't do that anymore. Even when it comes to raising kids, the fear-based approach to parenting no longer works. Neither does the "do it because I said so" approach, in which the manager (or parent, as the case may be) asserts his authority in a dictatorial way. Here's the problem: When you're on the receiving end, your only motivation to do something is to avoid getting punished. In this information age, both kids and adults are too smart for that. They want to understand *why* they're being asked to do something, whether it's eating their vegetables, practicing baseball fundamentals, or producing a business report in record time.

Therefore, as a manager you have to be reasonable, and you have to explain yourself. You have to demonstrate respect for your team players, no matter what kind of business you're in.

I have always respected authority. I was the youngest of five children growing up on Avenue T in East Flatbush, Brooklyn. I was showered with love by my older sisters Rae and Sister Marguerite, and given strong guidance by my older brothers Rocco and Frank. Rocco became a beat policeman and caring family man, and Frank became a professional ballplayer who made it to the big leagues as a first baseman for the Milwaukee Braves. As a kid, I twice witnessed him hitting home runs in the 1957 World Series against the Yankees, which were the most thrilling experiences of my early life. As I grew up and started playing ball myself, Frank was a terrific mentor, though a stern one. Both of my older brothers were solid, caring role models.

In addition to my mother and siblings, throughout my life I've had teachers and coaches who took an interest in me and helped me to develop a healthy concept of leadership. But I also had one glaringly negative role model: my father, Joe. He was a New York City detective who often terrorized our home with his out-of-control rages. While he never physically hit me, he verbally abused me, and he wielded his anger as a terrible weapon. (I know that my mother did not escape the back of his hand.)

After Frank, Rocco, and Sister Marguerite left our house, my sister Rae had terrible fights with my father, mostly as she attempted to defend my mother from his threats and actual attacks. During one intense scene, Rae must have felt so threatened that she grabbed a kitchen knife. He screamed at her to put down the knife, and when she didn't comply he turned and reached into a dining room drawer—the one that held his revolver. I did not know what he would do, but I was so frightened of my father that I felt he was capable of anything. I wasn't going to let this play out for one more second, so I grabbed the knife out of Rae's hand, put it down on the table, and yelled out some sort of nine-year-old challenge to my father to stop the insanity.

A few years later, when Frank was home during the minor league off-season, he insisted that my mother ask my father to leave, and with great courage he engineered an end to my father's reign of terror. Frank called us all together, laid down the law with my father, and helped ease his passage out of our home. Many years later, Frank, Rocco, Sister Marguerite, and I were able to find some way to reconcile with him, but none of us, save perhaps Sister Marguerite, were able to be really close to him.

My early history has had a profound influence on my life, in a variety of ways. One obvious one is that I can't stand loud noises. All the yelling, threats, and outbursts in my house left me with a permanent aversion to any kind of uproar. On the down side, I have usually shied away from confrontation, which may not have served me well in certain personal and work relationships. On the up side, I developed the strong moral sense that people should be civil to each other at home and in the workplace.

Throughout my years as a player, I had a hard time whenever coaches or managers used threats or screaming outbursts to intimidate players. I couldn't stand all that noise and disharmony. One of my managers with the Milwaukee Braves, Bobby Bragan, who is now a dear friend, could be a yeller. I recall one instance when I was sitting in the dugout, peering up into the stands looking for someone. Noticing this, Bobby shrieked at me, "Pay attention to the game!" I recall feeling totally embarassed in front of my teammates. In retrospect, I don't think what Bragan did was so terrible, but I was sensitive to that kind of humiliation and didn't like it. I might kid one of my players in similar circumstances, but I would do it in a low-key way so as not to humiliate.

I'm particularly sensitive to being embarassed in public. I don't want to get too psychoanalytical, but one incident with my father is most vivid. When I was about five or six, my parents had some friends over, and I went into the upstairs bathroom to urinate. Because I didn't close the door, the sound carried downstairs and was audible to the guests. My father must have been embarassed himself, and he flew into a vicious tirade at me in front of everyone, including my brother Frank, who later said he was afraid for me. This experience, and others, probably influenced me to embrace this guideline as a manager: Don't embarrass or humilate a team player in front of others. On very rare occasions, I will lose my temper and make an angry comment to a player within earshot of others, but I chalk this up to being human.

When I think about it, I can partly trace my managerial style to both the positive and negative influences in my early life. I revered my older brothers, and each presented different but compatible models of leadership: Rocco was warm and accessible, and Frank was a hard-driving mentor who always kept a flame under my ass. Without thinking it through, I've probably incorporated elements from both. At the same time, I rejected my father's way, because I saw how much pain he inflicted on my mother and all of his kids. I guess I emerged from childhood with an abiding respect for authority, but with a belief that with authority came the responsibility to be fair, moral, and decent to the people in your charge.

It all comes down to respect. To me, it's the golden rule: Treat others as you would wish to be treated.

Offer a Clean Slate

When I first come on a managerial job, or when new players join our team, I judge everyone from that day forward. Certain players come with baggage, but I try not to let it influence my dealings with them. When I was traded from the Atlanta Braves to the St. Louis Cardinals in the spring of 1969, I didn't think I carried any significant baggage. But I had been active as a union leader with the Braves, and apparently I developed a reputation that really wasn't deserved. About a year after I joined the Cards, I was named team captain, and someone in the oganization said, "You know, you're really not a troublemaker." I replied, "I didn't know I was one." I figured out that unfair rumors had been spread about me by the Braves' general manager, Paul Richards, perhaps as a reason to further justify their trading me.

My own experience is one reason I don't believe managers should prejudge people. A good example is Darryl Strawberry. I knew all about his checkered background—the substance abuse problems, family trouble, financial difficulties, conflicts with teammates, and his supposedly wasted potential. What was I supposed to do, ask him to do penance for all his past wrongdoings? My attitude was, he's with our club, and if I'm going to give someone a second chance—or even a third or fourth—I should start with him from the present onward, and forget about the past.

When Darryl first came to our team in the middle of the 1996 season, he strolled into my office and said, "Skip, anything you want me to do, just let me know." I realized right away that I could give Darryl the benefit of the doubt, and there was a decent chance he'd do his part. As it happened, he performed brilliantly through much of the 1996 Championship season, and he never complained about playing time, even though I platooned him in left field and did not always use him as my designated hitter. He was always composed, cooperative, and likeable. Gradually, he emerged as a team leader, and his status as a leader only grew through the 1997 and 1998 seasons.

Basically, Darryl had a good attitude when he first joined the Yankees, but I think it helped that he had a manager who offered a clean slate. I was receptive to his potential, he was receptive to my leadership, and Darryl thrived as a Yankee, both in terms of his behavior and his performance on the field. As of this writing, I don't know enough to comment about the incident that landed him in legal trouble at the start of the 1999 season. But I don't believe anyone should write off Darryl. He's a human being who has been under enormous stress, particularly given his diagnosis of colon cancer, the arduous chemotherapy treatments he's undergone, and the fact that his dream of returning to the Yankees had to be deferred.

Team players don't want to be prejudged. Executives and managers should offer that clean slate to employees with "reputations," because too often the rumors aren't true. Even if the rumors are true, people can change their ways—most often under firm and fair guidance from a manager. If workers don't live up to their commitments, or they don't give total effort, you can always read them the riot act. But there's no need to jump the gun; you'll only make them feel that they're fighting an uphill battle.

Don't Let Team Players Disrespect Each Other

Just as I offer players respect, I won't let them treat other members of the team with disrespect. In 1999, pitcher David "Boomer" Wells had a terrific season, with one highlight after another—a perfect game in May, being named starter for the American League in the All-Star game, a regular season record of 18–4, and a postseason record of 4–0. Boomer, a free spirit, was an inspiration to the 1998 team, but there were moments when his emotions got the best of him. On one occasion, in a mid-September game against the Baltimore Orioles, David showed a flash of disrespect to his teammates, and I had to talk to him about it immediately.

David was pitching smoothly until the sixth inning, when Danny Clyburn of the Orioles hit a towering pop fly to shallow left field. Derek Jeter and outfielders Ricky Ledee and Chat Curtis converged awkwardly, and the ball fell in for a bloop single. David put his hands on his hips, and he glared in the direction of his teammates. The ball probably should have been caught, but David moped on the mound in a way that wasn't appropriate. He lost his composure, promptly giving up three more singles. When I took him out of the game, he stomped angrily off the mound.

Boomer's body language concerned me. After the game, which we won 15–5, he and I had a brief chat. I let him know I hadn't liked what I had seen. David responded well; he realized that he had behaved unprofessionally, and he vowed to apologize to his teammates. I believe that he did apologize to them. He even chastised himself when he spoke to the media: "These guys have been making plays behind me all year and don't deserve that."

My purpose in talking to Boomer was to nip a potential problem in the bud. I can't allow players to berate each other, even in the heat of the moment. And David deserves credit for making amends with his teammates. As Tim McCarver suggests in his book with Danny Peary, *The Perfect Season,* Boomer, who never knew his father, likes to test people in authority. He'll push the limits to see what he can get away with, but in the end what he really wants is firm guidance.

In any organization, it's the manager's responsibility to set a respectful tone from the top. If you treat employees with regard, you're teaching them, by example, to treat one another with regard. This is crucial, because disrespect breeds divisiveness on any team. Whether you're in a super competitive business or in team sports, *winning is tough enough when you're all pulling together*. When you're pulling apart, you have no chance.

Trust: The Foundation of Teamwork

For an organization or team, trust is like the connective tissue that binds together the structures of the body. Without that tissue, you're going to fall to pieces. In order to commit to a team, you must have trust—of your teammates and your leaders.

Whether I'm speaking to Little Leaguers or upper-echelon corporate executives, I emphasize trust. Everything I've said about fairness and respect is relevant to trust: When you are evenhanded and respectful toward all your team players, you create a bond of trust with them. They, in turn, are more likely to create bonds of trust with each other.

Of course, you should trust with your eyes open. If people violate your trust, whether by breaking rules or giving less than full effort, you have to take action, whether that means a fine or a no-punches-pulled conversation. But if you operate on the "clean slate" premise, as I did with Darryl Strawberry, Dwight Gooden, David Wells, and other players with supposed baggage, you'll often reap what you sow in the trust department.

In the world of baseball, managerial trust refers to many things. It means that you trust your players to:

1. Follow the rules you have set down.
2. Treat management and teammates with respect.
3. Be prepared physically and mentally for your work/play.
4. Give total effort on the field of work/play.

5. Do whatever it takes to get the most out of their abilities.

Whether in sports or business, managers should offer trust to employees in all five of these areas. If you're a team player, be aware that the way to earn and keep your manager's trust is to fulfill each of these five points. In this regard, I've been unbelievably fortunate with the Yankees. I could count on one hand the number of players who have not earned my trust. In fact, I'd still have a few uncounted fingers left.

Most people outside the Yankees—fans, sportswriters, and others in media—acknowledge that I trust my players, and I've gotten mainly positive reactions to how I've put this philosophy into practice. But I have occasionally been criticized for trusting certain players too much, particularly when it comes to performance. I've left David Cone in many games, long past the time some observers felt was justified. Another good example is my loyalty to my left-handed ace, Andy Pettitte.

Andy has been vital to our starting rotation since I came to the Yankees in 1996. He throws a good cut fastball and sinker, though he can get in trouble when he doesn't keep the ball down in the strike zone. Overall, he's been remarkably consistent, with more wins over the last three seasons than any other pitcher in the American League, and a career-winning percentage—.657—that is second best among all active pitchers. But Andy struggled noticeably in the last two months of the '98 season and ended what began as a terrific year with a 16–11 record. He pitched well in the second game of our division series against Texas, securing a 3–1 victory, but he was ineffective in the third game against Cleveland in the ALCS. In that game, which we lost 6–1, Andy was rocked by four home runs. After we beat Cleveland to win our AL championship, I kept hearing suggestions that I leave Andy out of the World Series rotation entirely.

Deciding whether and when to pitch Andy in the Series was made more complicated by an unexpected development. Andy's father, Tom, became seriously ill and had to undergo double bypass heart surgery two days after we finished off the Indians in six games. (People wanted to know if I would have put the ball in Andy's hand for a final Game Seven against Cleveland, but I never had to make public my decision.) Andy went to Houston to be with his father, with whom he is extremely close. When we knew the surgery went well and Andy could shortly return, I realized that I could pitch him as early as Game Two of the World Series against the Padres.

But Andy was under stress, mainly due to his father's surgery. You can't ignore such personal events when they can affect a person's performance on the field. (I make certain to have information about players' personal difficulties when it's relevant to the team.) I also recognized that he put intense pressure on himself after his loss in Cleveland and his late-season troubles. Andy is wound very tight, always expecting too much of himself.

In making up my mind about the World Series rotation, I had to consider all these factors. Orlando Hernandez had been pitching phenomenally well—he'd gotten us out of the worst jam we faced all season when we were down two games to one against Cleveland, hurling seven brilliant innings of shutout ball in our Game Four victory. I decided to use Wells, Hernandez, Cone, and Pettitte—in that order—for the first four games against the Padres. I knew that Andy might consider this something of a demotion, since I'd always put him in the first, second, or third slot in my pitching rotation, so when I broke the news to him, I explained my reasoning.

I told Andy that I thought he needed a bit more time to feel comfortable about his father's condition. But I also had to be honest—we needed to go first with starters who were sharp right now, including Hernandez, to get an early edge in the series. "We're not dismissing you, we're just going with our hot hand," I said. "If the shoe was on the other foot, you'd understand why you were getting the nod." I thought Game Four would be the best spot for Andy—he'd have more rest and hopefully more reassurance about his dad's condition.

Andy was disappointed, but I think he understood my position. Meanwhile, there were media folks who seriously questioned whether I should pitch Pettitte at all. It was not the first time people accused me of being "too loyal" to Andy. But I would not have considered taking Andy out of the rotation, simply because I trust him. I had to remember that he'd won huge games for us in our 1996 Championship Series against Baltimore, and in Game Five of the World Series against Atlanta.

I trust Pettitte because I know he gives total effort, every time on the mound. If he has any fault, it's that he overprepares and tries too hard to be perfect. If he throws a bad sinker, he can get caught up trying to make adjustments. But this minor weakness is also a strength—I never have to worry whether Andy will be prepared, or whether he'll give every ounce of his arm and heart on the mound. With a team player like Andy, it's easy to be patient and trusting, even if he falls into a rut.

A good example of Pettitte's determination was his performance in the 1996 World Series. In our first game against the Braves at Yankee Stadium, Andy was shellacked for six hits and seven earned runs in a mere 2⅓ innings, and we lost 12–1. After losing the next game, we clawed our way back into the Series with two thrilling wins. Andy's next turn in the rotation came with the Series tied at two games apiece, and some wondered whether he would fold under the pressure.

But Andy is a gamer. Though he's prone to getting tight, when our backs are against the wall he seems to reach down and find something extra. I can't see this too well from the dugout, but people have observed that when Andy is locked in, he gets a burning look in his eyes, staring down batters from under the bill of his cap. In Game Five in Atlanta, a pitching duel against the Braves' brilliant John Smoltz, he had that look. Andy shut down the Braves' dangerous hitters, allowing only five hits and no runs through 8⅓ superb innings. We beat the Braves 1–0, which catapulted us back to Yankee Stadium for a Game Six, which would be our World Series championship victory.

As it happened, Andy would pitch Game Four of the '98 series after we'd beaten the Padres three straight, so he had the opportunity to be the winning pitcher in our final game. He would face the Padres' formidable Kevin Brown, who had had a great postseason and was being touted as unhittable. I'm sure it helped Andy that his father was released from the hospital earlier that day, but I'm also sure that his dad was still on his mind. I know what it's like to be thrust into a high-pressure playoff game when someone you love is going through a tough time. My brother Frank underwent his heart transplant operation on our day off before the final game of the 1996 World Series.

I was concerned that Andy hadn't pitched in twelve days. But in the first inning, my fears were allayed when I saw the first pitch come out of his hand so effortlessly. From that point on, it was vintage Pettitte. He had that look in his eyes again. He escaped from a bases-loaded jam in the second inning, and in the seventh he made a heads-up fielding play, grabbing a chopper off the bat of Carlos Hernandez, then catching Ruben Rivera halfway between second and third. Andy pitched into the eighth inning, giving up only five hits and no runs. We won the game 3–0, and we had our second World Series championship in three years.

My trust in Andy had been rewarded, and it's a lesson I have learned repeatedly as manager of the Yankees. When you have players with track records of hard work, grace under pressure, and key contributions to the team, you should grant them your trust—even if they've shown some inconsistency. Managers need employees with that much grit and talent. If you abandon them whenever they make mistakes, you'll lose *their* trust, which means you could lose their total commitment to the team effort.

Here, baseball is exactly like business or life. Employees and executives alike make mistakes, and they have uneven patches in their productivity. If you know from past history that they are creative and capable, you owe them the trust that they can return to form. Your sole requirement should be maximum effort.

By the same token, workers should grant managers the trust that their decisions are best for the team. If you resent every move by your manager that does not suit your individual goals, you'll erode your own commitment, which in the long term will damage both your individual performance and the team's potential for success. (For instance, if Pettitte had let his disappointment turn into a serious funk, he'd never have come through as he did in Game Four.) I've had to bench people I trust, like our first baseman Tino Martinez in several games in the 1996 World Series, but in the long-term he understood that I would not abandon him for long stretches. I trust Tino not only because he's a great ball-player, but because he's another guy who always gives 100 percent. Like Pettitte, Tino only gets in trouble when he makes excessive demands of himself, because he's such a per-fectionist. No doubt he was mad when I benched him in '96, but the anger didn't last long.

Defend Team Players Who Give Effort

Managers can show trust in many ways. One of the principles I live by is "Give me effort and I'll never second-guess you. I'll always defend you." In my world, this means defending players to the media and sometimes to others in the organization. Some sportswriters and commentators rush to judgment, and I consider it part of my job to counter harsh criticism as clearly and gracefully as I can.

In sports, media stories can be a real problem for team players. A premier ballplayer strikes outs twice and hits into a couple of double plays, and he's a an overpaid bum. But it's silly. Let's say the overpaid bum makes five million a year, but so does the pitcher he's batting against. Why should the five-million-dollar batter always beat the five-million-dollar pitcher, or vice versa? They can't both win the battle.

In baseball, the difference between a hitting slump and a hot streak comes down to this: The cold batter gets roughly two hits every ten at-bats (.200), while the hot batter gets three hits every ten at-bats (.300). While this is no small difference, the media can blow it out of proportion, and some guys become self-conscious at the plate, which only prolongs the slump. I'm not blaming the media, I'm only saying that I can ease the strain on players by making comments to the media that put a player's trouble in perspective. For instance, my center fielder Bernie Williams may strike out three times in a given game, but if he makes a brilliant catch to prevent a run, I remind reporters of his effort. I constantly make this point to both my players and the media: There's more than one way to contribute to team goals. Never overlook the sacrifice bunt, the heads-up baserunning play, the strike thrown from the outfield to nail an advancing runner.

I never take an adversarial tack with the media. Nor am I suggesting that team players cultivate an "us against them" attitude toward legitimate reporters. In fact, people give the media too much power by engaging in constant battles with them. But managers can lessen negative effects on team players by offering the media honest answers to tough questions, answers that remind everyone of the big picture. In this way, I act as a buffer, quenching the media's understandable thirst for information while keeping the heat off my players.

Although media coverage of business is increasing, a manager's vow to defend employees may be more relevant to criticism from higher-ups in the organization than from the press. Managers in most companies are more likely to hear the equivalent of "he's an overpaid bum" from upper-level executives or CEOs than from the media. I encourage managers at all levels in the corporate hierarchy to defend team players who've demonstrated hard work, good faith, and passionate commitment to the team. This helps create powerful bonds of trust between managers and team players, and among team players themselves. If you strengthen the connective tissue that keeps teams together, you'll be following one of the fundamental ground rules for winning.

Torre's Winning Ways
Key #2: Fairness, Respect, and Trust

- **Apply Fairness**
  - Be absolutely equitable in how you treat team players. Don't give an employee an extra edge based on pay scale, or reputation, or personal feelings rather than his or her performance.
  - Apply team rules and guidelines with utmost fairness.
  - Remember that managerial fairness builds teamwork and togetherness.

- **Grant Respect**
  - You've got to give respect to get it back.
  - Don't embarrass or humiliate team players in front of others.
  - Offer team players with "reputations" a clean slate. Rumors are often untrue; even when they are true, team players can transform themselves.
  - Don't let team players "dis" each other.

- **Cultivate Trust, the Foundation of Teamwork**
  - Managers should trust team players to fulfill these points, and team players should work to earn that trust:
    1. Follow the rules you have set forth.
    2. Treat management and teammates with respect.
    3. Be prepared physically and mentally for work/play.
    4. Give total effort on the field of work/play.
    5. Do whatever it takes to get the most of your own ability.
  - Let team players know that if they give maximum effort, you will always defend them inside and outside the organization.

CHAPTER 3 **Key #3:**

Straight Communication:

The Key to Trust

Every manager should feel that he can talk
to his team players. Every team player should feel that he can
talk to his manager. Communication is the key to trust, and
trust is the key to teamwork in any group endeavor, be it in
sports, business, or family. Smooth, open communication
helps us to get things done, accomplish goals, refine strategies, grease organizational wheels, and solidify relationships
at the heart of our work and family lives. Yet we often neglect
to learn new communication skills, because we underestimate their importance in our quest for success. Also, many of
us think that we can't learn how to communicate more effectively. But we *can* become better communicators, and when
we do, it plays a big part in realizing our dreams of winning.

I rely on certain basic guidelines for straight communication. These guidelines have worked during my sixteen years
of talking to team players individually and collectively. But
with the Yankees, I've had a group of players committed to
straight communication, and that's shown me how well a

team can function when people are that responsive and direct with each other.

Managers should know what employees need in the way of communication and support. They should sense when to initiate communication. They should acknowledge workers' fears and concerns. They should get conflicts out on the table. They should know when to talk and when to listen. They should use group communication when necessary, to air problems and re-energize the team. Likewise, team players should be honest, responsive, and straight with their manager and their colleagues.

Communication matters in every aspect of our work lives. In baseball, it matters in the clubhouse and on the field, at home, and on the road.

In one memorable instance, straight communication may have directly helped us to win a World Series. I'm talking about the 1996 Yankees, a team that persisted against the odds, again and again, through a postseason roller-coaster ride. After losing the first two games to the Atlanta Braves on our home turf, we found ourselves in a deep hole. We had not simply been beaten, we'd been trounced—by a combined score of 16–1. The Braves' starting pitchers were rightly feared; we'd been shut down by John Smoltz and Greg Maddux in Games One and Two, and now we would face the tough left-hander, Tom Glavine, in Game Three.

I had decided at the start of the World Series to save pitcher David Cone for Game Three in Atlanta's Fulton County Stadium. One reason was my belief that Game Three is often pivotal, and Cone is a true big-game pitcher. He operates on sheer guts and never backs down from a challenge. Back in May of that year, Cone was sidelined with circulatory problems in his arm that caused numbness in his hand, affecting his feel for the ball. He was diagnosed with an aneurysm in his armpit, a serious condition that required immediate surgery. It was a career-threatening injury, but Cone made a remarkable recovery. When he returned on September 2, a mere four months later, he threw seven innings of no-hit ball. As I got to know David during our first season together, I found that he was the consummate professional. He's a thoroughly committed, straightforward, and insightful team player, one I could rely on as a leader and an inspritation to the team.

We *had* to beat the Braves in Game Three (no team has come back from a 3–0 deficit in the World Series). With Cone as my starter, I knew we had a chance. And he didn't disappoint: through the first five innings, he was pitching a three-hit shutout. We led, 2–0, as David took the mound in the sixth inning. Throughout the '96 season, the sixth inning was often critical. That was because of "the formula." As the regular season progressed, it became clear that our flame-throwing middle reliever, Mariano Rivera, could shut teams down at will for two innings, the seventh and eighth. With a lead in the ninth, I'd bring in our hard-throwing closer, John Wetteland, who'd established himself as one of the best in the majors. The "formula" was therefore pretty simple: Hold a lead through six, and blank the opponent with Rivera and Wetteland for the last three innings.

If Cone could get three outs in the sixth, I was confident we'd have our World Series victory, and a real chance to come back from the brink. But the inning began with an ominous development: He walked pitcher Tom Glavine. Marquis Grissom singled, Mark Lemke popped out trying to bunt, and Chipper Jones walked. The bases were loaded with one out, and David seemed to be losing his command. My right-handed ace was faltering, and he was going to face two dangerous left-handed hitters: Fred McGriff, their most potent threat; and Ryan Klesko.

How crucial was this situation? The Braves were in a position to blow us out of the water with one swing of the bat. I saw this as a turning point in the Series—the difference between being down two games to one with a chance to climb back, and being down three games to zero with virtually no chance. As I look back, I realize that I had to make a life-or-death baseball decision: Do I stick with a tiring David Cone, or do I play the percentages and bring in my left-handed relief specialist, Graeme Lloyd, to face the two lefty threats? As I jogged out to the mound, I had no idea what my decision would be.

In theory, I had no problem leaving Cone in the game. In his career, he'd already proven his big-game ability, and I wasn't afraid to let him face McGriff, or any left-hander—as long as he wasn't drained. But I had to know whether he had anything left in his arm. There was only one person who knew whether David could deliver in this situation, and that was David.

My decision to let him pitch or bring in Lloyd would depend solely on how he answered my question. I needed the truth, and nothing but the truth. I purposely stuck my face a few inches from his, and looked straight into his eyes. He looked straight back into mine. As we locked stares, catcher Joe Girardi, standing right next to us, seemed miles away, and the fifty thousand fans in Fulton County Stadium disappeared. "This is very important," I said. "You have to tell me the truth. How do you feel?"

"I'm OK," he said. "I lost the feel on my slider a bit, but I'll get this guy for you."

It sounded good, but I wasn't satisfied yet. I was balancing two realities in my mind: one, that David is a relentless bulldog, a hungry competitor who always wants the ball; and two, that David is a straight-shooter. The only time he might ever stretch the truth would be to keep himself out on the mound. I had to make sure that I was talking to the straight-shooter, not the guy who'll say anything to stay in the game.

"This game is too important," I shot back. "I have to know the truth, so don't bullshit me."

Without hesitating, Cone said, "I can get him. I can get out of this inning."

I liked his answer, and more than that, I liked the unwavering look in his eyes. "Let's go get 'em," I said, and I walked off the mound, leaving the ball in Cone's hand. There's something inside the great ones that enables you to trust them more.

McGriff was the key. I knew if Cone could get him for the second out, we'd probably escape the inning with our lead intact. If he couldn't get McGriff, I'd have to pull him. David threw a hard first strike, then McGriff popped out to the infield. I breathed a huge sigh of relief. I was concerned but not alarmed when he walked Klesko to force in a run, because he still appeared strong and confident. With two outs, and the score now 2–1, Cone's confrontation with Javy

Lopez would be the final test of my decision and David's resolve. With one strike against him, Lopez popped up in foul territory. Joe Girardi made the grab for the final out, and I felt in my gut that we would win this game and fight our way back in the Series. We *did* win Game Three, by a score of 5–2, and it would indeed be the turning point in our come-from-behind World Series championship.

My exchange on the mound with Cone, which I'll never forget, brought together several ground rules. Because I knew my player, I was able to accurately gauge his response. I realized that the only time David Cone would stretch the truth would be to stay in a game, but I also knew that his basic honesty would take precedence if I *demanded* the truth. Ultimately, it was a moment on the field of play in which winning depended on straight communication.

Most often, however, winning depends on off-the-field communication. How do we talk to each other during a typical work day? How do managers deal with interpersonal conflicts, motivational lapses, and strategic planning? Whether in baseball, the workplace, or the family, we can't accomplish much in these areas without straight communication. If we've established an open dialogue in our daily interactions, we'll be able to sustain it on the field of play, too. For instance, in the business world, coworkers, managers, and executives who communicate well in the workplace will be better prepared when they make boardroom presentations or meet with clients. The team concept they've built behind the scenes will carry over when team members are required to perform effectively as a unit on their own particular "field of play."

Here are my five guidelines to straight communication, applicable in the workplace or on the field:

1. Identify individual needs: Figure out what each individual needs in the way of communication, be it support, motivation, technical help, or the proverbial "kick in the ass."

2. Time your talks: Determine when the "door is open" for communication with a particular team player. Know when you have to nudge it open with helpful or directive comments.

3. Acknowledge emotions: Let team players know that you accept the range of their emotions, including fear, uncertainty, and anxiety.

4. Get issues out on the table: Managers and team players must be able to air grievances and deal with problems in an open manner, respectfully but without holding back. Otherwise, conflicts and resentments fester, sapping motivation and undermining teamwork.

5. Use team talk to ventilate and motivate: Managers can use team meetings to air problems and motivate groups and individuals.

In the following section, "Person to Person: The Building Blocks of Trust," I will explain the first four guidelines, which relate to individual communication between managers and team players. In the final section, "Use Team Talk to Ventilate and Motivate," I explain the fifth guideline, which reveals how managers can use team meetings most effectively.

Person to Person: The Building Blocks of Trust

Baseball is different from most other team sports in one important aspect. Individual performance is more important in baseball, because what a batter does at the plate, what a pitcher does on the mound, or what a fielder does when a ball comes his way, depends almost solely on the batter, the pitcher, and the fielder—no one else. The batter is alone at the plate, and so is the pitcher on the mound and the fielder at his position; all of them are called on to do their jobs through their own autonomous efforts. (The one partial exception is the pitcher, who depends on the catcher to call pitches, and sometimes to influence an umpire's call by "framing" the pitch. But it still comes down to whether a pitcher has good stuff, which the catcher can't do anything about.) Basketball and football depend more heavily on teamwork on the field of play. Set plays in basketball can determine whether the team's best shooter gets his best shot. In football, the carefully choreographed movements of the linemen will determine whether the running back has a hole to run through.

Teamwork in baseball is mostly behind-the-scenes. When ballplayers are motivated to perform to the best of their ability because they know the guys next to them in the clubhouse are depending on them, that's teamwork. When ballplayers care enough about each other to embrace the shared goal of winning with solid commitment, that's teamwork. When one guy is slumping at the plate and others in the lineup pick up the slack, that's teamwork. The 1998 Yankees showed what's possible in baseball with optimal teamwork.

Because baseball is such an autonomous sport, creating teamwork depends more on communication between individuals rather than the entire group. In other words, since I need maximum *individual* effort from my starting pitchers, my relievers, and my hitters, I have to establish good communication with each team member. I therefore rely on person-to-person encounters to motivate, give players a chance to share concerns, or just shoot the breeze in order to know them better. If the model I present of straight communication influences players to talk more openly and respectfully with one another, all the better. In terms of the manager's role as a communicator, I think that baseball and business are very much alike.

That's why the following four guidelines focus on person-to-person communication.

Identify Individual Needs

This guideline rests upon Key #1: Know Your Team Players. When you follow the "make time doctrine" in order to know your players, you'll be able to identify what each one needs in the way of communication.

Every team player needs something unique. Often, my first baseman, Tino Martinez, must be reminded of his many contributions; center fielder, Bernie Williams, needs reassurance; starting pitcher, Hideki Irabu, needs a friendly kick in the butt; right fielder, Paul O'Neill, needs a light touch to offset his frustrations. (Occasionally, these individuals need other kinds of communication, too, which only shows that team players need different things at different times.) Moreover, I might say the same thing to four different people, but I'll say it in a different way—my tone or style will depend on who I'm dealing with.

Getting to know employees will enable you to identify individual needs for communication. Then you can most effectively use the communication skills I emphasize here: timing your talks, acknowledging emotions, getting issues on the table, and knowing when to talk and when to listen.

I love my center fielder, Bernie Williams, an enormously gifted outfielder and powerful switch-hitter who is also a person of real depth. The way Bernie carries himself, with quiet dignity and intelligence, reminds me of the late tennis star Arthur Ashe. He's also a talented musician who plays rock and classical guitar, and he's been known to write poetry in his spare time in the clubhouse or on the road—not your typical ballplayer hobbies. When I describe Bernie as high maintenance, I don't mean it in a negative way. Because Bernie is low-key and introspective, I need to converse with him regularly just to know where his head is every day. Not anything intense, necessarily—it's often enough for me to pass him as he strides toward center field during practice and make a lighthearted remark—"Bernie, are you with us today?" He'll stare back at me and play along. "Yeah, I'm fine, I'm doing OK." It's an opening—if anything happens to *not* be OK, he'll have a chance to tell me.

Tino Martinez is a tenacious ballplayer who, like Andy Pettitte, Paul O'Neill, and several others in our club, becomes intensely frustrated whenever he's not jumping the high bar he's set for himself. It's one of the traits I most respect about Tino, but it can cause him trouble. In early 1998, Tino was on a hot streak when he was hit by a pitch in the middle of his upper back, causing a deep injury. He didn't go on the disabled list, but his ability to swing the bat was clearly impaired. He wasn't right for about a month. I recognized that despite his physical difficulty, Tino still wasn't cutting himself any slack, and I thought he needed to ease up on himself.

There was one game during this period when Tino made a diving grab for a ball down the first-base line that saved a run. We won the game, but he was seething because he hadn't gotten a hit. I made it a point to say, "Tino, nice going." He answered under his breath, "Yeah, nice going, I stink." I persisted. "But you helped us win the game with that play." He still didn't buy it, but I'd made my point. It's one I've made repeatedly to him: Even when you're slumping at the plate, you can make other contributions that matter. My communications with Tino contain two underlying messages. The first message is "Lighten up on yourself." The second message is "I'm in your corner; I believe in you."

One of your tasks as a manager is to send positive messages to a team player who undercuts himself with that kind of negative thinking. (If I wrote off players who got down during slumps, I'd be writing off some of my most valuable guys.) You can't be a psychologist, but you can be a supportive presence for your employees. As a manager, a high level of sensitivity will help you make snap decisions about what to say, how to say it, and when to say it. Some of your players require unconditional support. Others need to be massaged. Still others need to be pushed to work harder. Everyone needs attention.

Sometimes, a word of appreciation is enough. In 1998, we had a terrific bench player, Homer Bush, who has since been traded to the Blue Jays in the deal for Roger Clemens. Homer's primary role was as a pinch-runner. He's not only fast, he has extraordinary instincts as a baserunner, always making something happen with his aggressiveness. When he'd try to steal, Homer wouldn't just run, he'd explode on his jump, then slide head-first into second or third. "You've got larceny in your soul," I once told him admiringly. Apparently, my comment made an impression on Homer. Early in his 1999 season with Toronto, he got picked off at first base. The next time he was in a position to steal, he noticed that he was tentative. A voice in his head kept repeating, "Should I go, should I not go?" Homer says that in the midst of his indecision, he remembered what I said to him, and he instantly stopped being hesitant. He claims that he's been fine on the base paths ever since.

Time Your Talks

You've had an argument with your spouse, and you both need time to cool off. In the meantime, you figure out what you want to say to patch it up. But you've learned one thing for certain: If you don't find the right time to say it, all your good intentions will go up in smoke. Anyone who's been married or lived with a partner knows what I mean. If you don't wait long enough, your spouse, still smoldering, either won't hear you, or will misinterpret what you have to say. Wait too long, and you've lost your opportunity.

The same holds true for a manager's talks with his team players. Timing is everything. Once you've identified the kind of communication needed, you've got to determine the best time to have that talk. Your decision must be based on your gut sense of when he or she is receptive. You might know exactly the right thing to say, but if the door is closed it won't make a bit of difference.

Derek Jeter is amazingly consistent as both a fielder and a hitter, but even he has occasional dry spells. In June of '98, Derek strained an abdominal muscle and had to go on the disabled list for several weeks. After he returned, he cooled down considerably at the plate, struggling to shake off the rust. His batting average when he went on the DL was .329; within ten days it had dropped twenty-three points. I didn't say anything to Derek right away; I waited until I sensed that he really wanted some words from me. Had I spoken too soon it would have shown a lack of confidence; forcing the issue would have been intrusive. Well into his dry spell, Derek sat down next to me in the dugout, and I figured the time was right.

Young players like Derek, full of pride and spunk, are by nature impatient. When he was slow coming back to form, he got even tighter and more self-conscious swinging the bat. I know this problem well from my years as a player, so it's easy for me to share some wisdom. "It's a timing mechanism you can't rush," I told Jeter. "It'll come back to you. Don't fight yourself, just let it happen. Keep working at it, and it will come back."

I think Derek appreciated my comments; they seemed to take some weight off his shoulders. They also demonstrated my confidence in him, which happens to be boundless. Within a few days, Derek went on a hitting tear, batting .400

during a five-game winning streak. He ended the season batting .324, fifth best in the American League. Derek would have emerged from his slump without a word from me, but it's possible that our talk helped to hasten his return to form. Even when managers can't make a direct impact on player performance, they can strengthen their bonds with players by showing their interest.

It's one of those true clichés that we can learn more from losing than winning. But for team players to learn from loss, they usually need to talk about it. If they don't, the feeling of defeat can fester until it ruins their self-confidence. Managers in any field need to provide the proper perspective about loss. Corporations can train managers and executives to empower team players to learn from disappointment or failure. But here again, it comes down to timing. Preach this message in the hours after a stinging failure, and your team member might not hear you. Some players will be receptive a day later, others will need months.

My ace reliever, Mariano Rivera, experienced one of those huge disappointments. In 1997, as we tried to repeat our '96 triumph, we faced the Indians in the best-of-five division series. Ahead two games to one, we were poised to finish them off in Game Four and head to the ALCS. Behind solid pitching by Dwight Gooden, we had a 2–1 lead going into the eighth. Five outs away from winning the series, I brought in Mariano to complete the job. With two outs in the eighth, Mariano faced the clutch hitter Sandy Alomar. Rivera has a blazing 95-mile-an-hour fastball that rises over the plate, but he fell behind two balls and no strikes. It appeared to me that Mo tried to throw the next pitch for a strike, but did not rely on his better fastball. Alomar slugged the pitch for an opposite field home run, tying the game 2–2. Ramiro Mendoza gave up the go-ahead run in the ninth, and we were forced to play Game Five against the Indians. We lost that heart-breaker 4–3, and with it our hopes for another world championship.

Giving up the series-altering home run to Alomar was hard for Rivera to swallow. In some ways, Mariano was a victim of his own talent—he's such a reliable reliever that everyone takes for granted his ability to shut the door in these situations. Mariano blamed himself for the loss, and I didn't want him carrying this albatross around his neck. But I waited until we left Cleveland to say anything. When we got off the airplane, I pointedly told Mariano what a wonderful year he had, that he was one of the main reasons we'd gotten as far as we had.

During spring training of '98, I could tell that the Alomar home run was still eating away at Mariano. So pitching coach Mel Stottlemyre and I sat down and had a talk with him. My philosophy about such events is this: I'd rather talk about it outright than whisper about it. I hoped that our conversations would help Mariano put the incident behind him. All I can tell you is that he pitched magnificently throughout the 1998 regular season, and flawlessly in the playoffs and World Series. In the thirteen innings Mariano pitched in the '98 postseason, he did not allow a single earned run. You can't do better than a 0.00 ERA.

Occasionally, managers have to force the timing of an important conversation or point of information. Tino Martinez, for example, might not always seem receptive to hearing from me about his positive defensive contributions while he's having offensive woes. But I make my comments anyway, because I think he needs to hear them and I need to say them.

I see no difference between the need for well-timed communication in the world of baseball and the world of business. Managers must refine and use their judgment about how and when to initiate an exchange with an employee. Likewise, workers can initiate dialogue with managers, supervisors, or executives, about any issue or concern, as long as they use the same care and judgment.

Acknowledge Emotions

In sports, business, and life, we're realizing that it's pointless to pretend we're not afraid when we are afraid, to plaster on a smile when we're in the throes of grief. As I've matured as a manager and a person, it's become clear to me that we can't be brave if we're not afraid. Think about it: How can we even *know* that we're brave unless we've felt and faced fear?

We're not robots, and we demonstrate courage when we persevere *despite* our fears. That doesn't mean we push our anxieties under the rug. Instead, we can admit to them and get on with our business. It's a more honest way to live and work, and it brings us together with fellow team players who are just as human as we are. I see a change in the world of sports: Grown men cry and talk about their fears where once they were cool at all costs. There's a time and place for stoicism in sports and life, but we should strike a balance between expressing emotions and keeping them private.

Key #3: Straight Communication: The Key to Trust

It makes sense to stay emotionally controlled on the field of play, whether you're standing on a baseball diamond, at a conference podium, meeting-room lectern, or on a theatrical stage. (I'm known for staying cool in the dugout, a point I'll return to in chapter 4.) When you've got to perform, you must be focused on the job at hand. But behind the scenes—in the clubhouse, boardroom, office suite, or rehearsal hall—you should be freer to acknowledge and communicate your genuine thoughts and feelings.

For instance, I'll try to make sure that Bernie Williams talks to me about what's going on with him. In our 1997 divisional series against Cleveland, we faced a final do-or-die Game Five after our tough loss in Game Four. We fell behind 4–0, but on the brink of elimination we came back, reminding ourselves of all the come-from-behind wins we'd engineered in the miraculous '96 postseason. Bernie Williams drove in two runs with a well-timed single, and we'd cut the Indians lead to 4–3. We entered the top of the ninth believing we would seize the moment once again.

We faced the Indian's closer, Jose Mesa, who got two quick ground-ball outs by Tim Raines and Derek Jeter. But up came Paul O'Neill, who drilled a Mesa pitch to deep right-center field, where it hit the bottom of the wall—a few feet from tying the game. Bernie Williams came to bat, with two outs and the tying run at second base. Bernie had had a rough series until that earlier RBI single, and I suppose he saw this as his chance for total redemption. One base hit, and we'd have a shot at another October miracle.

Bernie went after the first pitch from Mesa. He hit a solid fly ball to left-center, but it was easily caught by the Indians' left fielder, Brian Giles. Our entire season had come to a sudden, screeching halt.

I decided to have a team meeting, right away, to help my players deal with the disappointment. On my way from the dugout to the clubhouse, I passed Bernie, who was sitting on the steps and feeling really down. It was obvious that Bernie had taken the loss on his shoulders, since he'd made the last out. I said, "Bernie, it doesn't always work out the way you want it to. We wouldn't have been in the game if it hadn't been for you." He joined the rest of the team, whom I addressed in a similar way. I told them I was proud of the way they played, and I thanked them for their hard work all season.

But Bernie was still upset. We both knew it, and there was no sense pretending otherwise. It was better for Bernie to let me know how he felt than to maintain a false front. At the very least, it made me aware that I had more work to do. I spoke to him again a few weeks later, and he was still troubled by his "failure." "Bernie, good things won't happen every time you swing the bat," I said. "I know it seemed that way in 'ninety-six. But sometimes, the other guy is going to do better than you. You can't win every battle."

I think Bernie got the message and I believe that such conversations can help team players to put their losses behind them. You can't get past a serious loss or failure if you pretend it never happened, or that it didn't affect you. That's why I think it's so important for managers and workers in every sector of business and life to acknowledge the emotions stirred up by any situation, because that understanding is essential to communicating effectively.

I've talked with second baseman Chuck Knoblauch about the pressure he feels to produce at the plate. I've spoken to reliever Jeff Nelson about how down he gets when he doesn't deliver in tense late-game situations. And I've talked to our young catcher, Jorge Posada, about how anxious he gets when he's in a slump. I couldn't make much progress with these guys if they always concealed their emotions. Paul O'Neill, for one, is totally out front with his frustration and rage. Like Tino, when he doesn't hit, he berates himself, saying "I stink"—which couldn't be further from the truth. In early 1999, Paul was enduring one of his worst slumps when he turned to me and said, tongue-in-cheek, "Know how I can get my hands on some Prozac?"

Get Issues Out on the Table

When I was younger, I tended to hide from difficult, painful issues, whether they involved loved ones or colleagues in baseball. I found out the hard way just how important it is to deal with problems head-on. During my childhood, my father cast a darkness on our family with his rages, and I had survived by staying out of harm's way. I'd do anything to avoid him. It followed that as a young man I'd do anything to avoid confrontations with other people in my life. But I suffered from these early mistakes, and now I believe it's best to clear the air of conflict as swiftly and openly as possible. I've learned that confrontation doesn't have to be frightening or violent; you can confront people in a determined, respectful way. And you can hear what others have to say without getting defensive.

Whether I'm speaking to schoolchildren or corporate audiences, I always come back to three simple words about personal conflicts at home or at work: *Deal with it.*

Teamwork depends partly on how we handle conflict and trouble at work. If we gloss over every problem with an employee, colleague, or supervisor, we're going to live with that tension constantly. If we always say, "I'll deal with it tomorrow," we're asking for a tough night's sleep. I know, because I've had my share of sleepless nights.

There's only one surefire way to resolve conflicts with people in the workplace or the family: Get those troublesome issues on the table as soon as possible, and deal with them forthrightly. When you follow this advice, bear in mind my first three guidelines for communication: identify individual needs, time your talks, and acknowledge emotions. And do your best to bring to your dialogue these three qualities: clarity, honesty, and civility. You can express anger, even use tough language on occasion, but you don't have to lose control. In my book, screaming tantrums are not only a turnoff, they're not very effective.

In 1998, David Wells had a sensational year, but there were a few times when he and I had to resolve problems. There's no question that David brought immense energy and excitement to our season, that he raised his game to new heights, and that he came through brilliantly in the postseason. It's no secret that Boomer is a bird of a different feather, but that's always been part of his rough charm. At 6' 4" and 240 pounds, he's a big man with equally big appetites, and he had a powerful identification with Babe Ruth. He collected Ruth memorabilia and wanted nothing more than to wear Ruth's retired number 3 on the back of his pin-striped uniform. (He settled for 33.) David was raised near San Diego by a devoted single mother, Eugenia Ann (known as "Attitude Annie"), and one of his surrogate dads was a Hell's Angel. Maybe that explains his fascination with heavy metal music and his "born to be wild" attitude.

My view is that you have to accept people as they are. The Yankee players, coaches, and I accepted Boomer, which meant taking the good with the not-so-good. The good were his passion, sense of humor, and basic decency, not to mention his fastball. The not-so-good were his occasional lapses into lazy work habits and his moods. But I was able to deal with Boomer because Boomer was open to dealing with me.

A case in point was an incident in early May in a game against the Texas Rangers in Arlington. It was May 6, to be precise, and we staked Boomer to a 9–0 lead by the second inning. But David fell apart, allowing seven runs in the bottom of the second and third innings. With two outs in the third, he yielded a two-run homer to Mike Simms, and I had seen enough. What worried me as much as his sudden loss of control and velocity was his body language. He was circling and kicking the pitcher's mound, and generally proceeding at a snail's pace. When I went to take him out, he flipped the ball into my hand without meeting my eye, and stalked off the mound.

The press made it seem that I was furious with Wells for disrespecting me. That wasn't my problem. No pitcher is going to be happy coming out of a game when he had a 9–0 lead. I was concerned about his pitching collapse—the fact that he'd lost his command, his composure, and, seemingly, his energy in the ninety-eight-degree weather. I thought he would benefit by losing some weight, but I was more worried about his focus than his weight.

Three days later in Minnesota, I held a meeting with David and pitching coach Mel Stottlemyre to discuss the incident, and to talk about our general concerns about his performance. We told David that we wanted him to work harder, to be more mentally and physically prepared, and to never quit during the course of any game.

David listened to what we had to say, and then—most important—we listened to what he had to say. "I feel like you don't show confidence in me," he said flatly. David saw signs that he read as lack of faith on our part—such as warming up relievers too quickly or removing him from games too soon. Though I didn't think we'd shown a lack of confidence in him, that didn't matter. What mattered was that he *felt* that way, and I had to take that into account. As both player and manager, I have known exactly what it means to feel that your superiors are not demonstrating their confidence.

We reassured David that we valued his abilities, but wanted more effort from him. "Physically, you're our strongest pitcher," I said. "If you work hard and focus, you could be a leader on our staff." We made it clear that the stakes were high—if he reached his potential, he could become a focal point on a team that could go all the way.

It was a valuable give and take—and I emphasize give and take. It was vital that he hear our point of view, and equally vital that we hear his. Both sides came away with something. After our meeting I saw evidence that he was becoming a tougher competitor during his starts. For my part, I would wait a little longer before getting a reliever to warm up in the bullpen. He wanted us to show more confidence in him, so that's what we did.

Our conversation was a good example of the dialogue all managers can have with their team players. Make room for a genuine back-and-forth exchange. Be willing to consider the other guy's position. Demonstrate respect and trust in the way in which you hold the dialogue. Finally, you must take action on what you've learned, as David did by working harder, and we did by exhibiting more faith in him.

Boomer's next start at Yankee Stadium, against the Kansas City Royals, began inauspiciously. We quickly went ahead, 2–0, on a two-run homer by Bernie Williams, but Boomer labored in the first three innings and the Royals tied the score. Just when it seemed he would lose control of the game, he became even more determined, and got into groove with his pitches. Pitching into the eighth inning, David retired his last ten batters in a row; eight of his last fifteen outs were strikeouts. It looked like Boomer was doing everything he could to right the boat.

Boomer's next start, against the Minnesota Twins at Yankee Stadium on May 17, was unforgettable. Before every game, Stottlemyre observes the starter warming up, and offers a few words of advice. Before the game, I usually ask Mel his impression of the starter's warm-up session. I clearly recall his comments on May 17. "Wow," he said. "Boomer was scary."

With 49,820 fans in attendance for Beanie Baby Day, David ambled to the mound. The crowd got a lot more than Beanie Babies. We witnessed Boomer at his best, with pinpoint control and terrific movement on his fastball, curveball,

sinker, and changeup. As it dawned on us that he was working on a perfect game, the tension gripped everyone in the
dugout. David Cone sank deep into his jacket, right up to his
dark sunglasses. There's an age-old baseball superstition that
you don't talk to a pitcher when he's working on a no-hitter.
But by the seventh, Boomer seemed desperate for someone
in the dugout to break the ice. Cone went over to him and
wisecracked, "I think it's time to break out the knuckleball,"
which got a laugh and a deep breath out of Boomer.

Wells was so sharp that he only had a three-ball count on
four hitters, and only two balls were hit hard the entire afternoon. By the ninth, he still had not yielded a hit or a walk,
and the crowd was delirious at every pitch. He retired John
Shave on a fly ball to Paul O'Neill in right, then struck out
Javier Valentin. David would later say that his fingers were
numb to the final pitch, which was slapped into right field by
Pat Meares. The fly ball landed in the glove of O'Neill, and
David pumped his fist in the air. His teammates surrounded
him, lifting him on their shoulders as he celebrated to the
deafening sound of cheers from every fan in the stadium. He
was only the fifteenth pitcher in major league history to pitch
a perfect game, the first by a Yankee in the regular season.
The only other Yankee to achieve pitching perfection had
been Don Larsen, in the 1956 World Series against Brooklyn
(I remember it well; I was a high school student sitting in the
stands at Yankee Stadium). I felt great for Boomer, who will
take this accomplishment with him wherever he goes.

I can't claim that our meeting eleven days earlier laid the
groundwork for David's historic accomplishment. But I do
think he became more intense and committed to pitching

excellence. He also became more comfortable with his relationship with me and the coaching staff. These factors clearly helped Boomer. Also, pitching the perfect game became a motivator in itself. From then on, the media paid much closer attention to every start by Wells. He had something monumental to live up to, and he kept working hard to improve. David ended the season with an 18–4 record and a 3.49 ERA, and was widely recognized as one of the best pitchers in one of baseball's greatest years.

Our meeting with David illustrates how valuable it is for managers to get issues out on the table. It ends the whispering and hidden resentments. It helps managers and team players understand each other better. It enables everyone to put conflicts to rest so they can get on with the business of working and winning. But again, managers and team players alike should bring clarity, honesty, and civility to their dialogue. They should try for a give-and-take exchange, in which each side gets heard and respected. Don't mince words, but don't use words to mince the other guy.

One of the hardest things for any manager to do is release a team player, or move him to another location. In baseball, managers may be called upon to tell players that they've been sent to the minors or traded to another team. It can be excruciating when it comes time to break the news. I had that experience in February 1999, when I had to tell David Wells he had been traded, along with Graeme Lloyd and Homer Bush, to the Toronto Blue Jays for Roger Clemens. The decision to trade Wells in a package deal for Clemens had not been hard from a baseball perspective, since Clemens is a future Hall of Famer, possibly the greatest pitcher of his generation. But it was very hard from a personal perspective, since Wells had been so much a part of our remarkable '98 season, and since we knew how deeply he appreciated being a Yankee.

An essential part of my philosophy of straight communication is that I tell players myself that they've been moved or traded. It's tough, but you can't allow a messenger to carry that message for you. You've got to be able to look someone in the eye and tell him your decision. If you don't, you're not going to feel very good about yourself as a leader. At the very start of spring training in '99, on the day I was slated to tell David and Graeme Lloyd about the trade, I was up at 6 A.M., dreading the moment. Yankee general manager Brian Cashman and I called David into my office to break the news. He didn't know what was up when he joked, "What, the first day and I'm in the principal's office already?"

When we told him about the trade, Boomer was clearly in shock. "I know you've been such a devoted Yankee," I said. "But at least your stop here was memorable. Now you have the '98 season, and it's something you can take with you wherever you go." I was thinking of his perfect game, his pitching excellence, his World Series ring, the whole ball of wax. So was David when he said, "These were the best two years of my life." He was still stunned, and couldn't seem to leave the office, so we brought in Graeme Lloyd to tell him about the trade. (Homer Bush would not report till later that day.) Lloyd was devastated. I thanked David for our 1998 World Series ring, and I thanked Graeme for our 1996 and 1998 rings, since I believe that every team player was responsible for our championships. I gave each a hug and said, "I'm glad that both of you played such big parts in what we did last year."

I know that Wells took quite a while to recover from the trade. It took time for New York to recover, as well. Boomer is such a fiery spirit, and New Yorkers loved his combativeness, just as they loved Billy Martin's. But while Roger Clemens is an entirely different personality, he's a relentless competitor and a total professional, not to mention a genius of a pitcher.

It's hard to let anyone go, no matter how much money they make. It's especially tough when I have to break the news to players who may never find work on another team. I recall one such incident, with Gerald Perry, a first baseman and designated hitter who played for me in both Atlanta and St. Louis. In early 1995, I had to let Gerald know that we were releasing him. That was very hard, because he was a good person and a hard-working player who'd taken a lot of pride in his play.

I asked him to come to my office. "Gerald, we're going to have to cut you," I said. "But it's very difficult, because I love having you around and I think you're a class act. I just don't feel we have any other choice right now." Gerald made this rough moment easier for me; the best ones always do. But I tried to make it a little less painful for both of us by letting him know how highly I regarded him.

In the corporate world, most people—save high-level executives or CEOs with golden parachutes—have real financial insecurities and fears about their future when they've been pink-slipped. When you're in a position to fire or demote someone, you do yourself and the other person a favor by carrying out this difficult task with as much human-ity and decency as you can. When appropriate, you can also offer a strong reference and the promise to do whatever pos-sible to help in his or her job search.

When you must release an employee, I recommend these guidelines, under the "get issues out on the table" category:

1. Whenever possible, break the news yourself.
2. Be straightforward and take responsibility for the decision. Don't put the blame on someone else, as in "I wanted to keep you, but he didn't."
3. Thank the team player for his or her contributions.
4. Don't break the news in a mechanical way because you feel bad about what you're doing. Show some compassion, because you know how you'd feel in his or her shoes.

Use Team Talk to Ventilate and Motivate

Conventional wisdom says that you can't have enough team meetings. You'd think that corporate managers, team leaders, and upper-level executives have nothing to lose when they call the team together in one big room to deal with problems, plan strategies, and whip up motivation.

In my view, team meetings have their place, but they're like chili peppers—a few add zest to your dish; too many and you're asking for trouble. I don't like to call many team meet-ings, for several reasons. The first reason is specific to base-ball, which as I've said, is a more a game of individuals than most other team sports. Since individual performance is at the heart of the game, I often spend more time addressing each player and his problems than the team as a unit. That's been my experience and my preference. The second reason is that when a baseball manager calls a team meeting, it's like ringing an alarm bell: It signifies real trouble and you want everyone to pay close attention. If you ring the bell too often, the team won't take you or your meetings as seriously as they should.

There are agencies, firms, and companies that rely more heavily on orchestrated teamwork than we do in baseball. These organizations require regular staff meetings, so in this regard, I can't easily translate from baseball to business. But the fewer-is-better rule holds in several respects. When managers use team meetings to resolve group problems rather than to strategize, they should be careful about the alarm-bell problem. Countless gatherings, whether for the purpose of bawling out team players for poor performance or lighting a motivational fire, will lose their impact pretty fast. It's even possible to overdo strategic meetings, especially when they prevent actual work from getting done.

Yet in every organization, there is a place for the well-timed, well-conceived team meeting. During our record-breaking '98 season, we had two team meetings that helped us to stay on the winning track. One took place the very first week of the season, after we'd lost four of our first five games on the road. The other took place in mid-September, when our play was downright sluggish, and I did not want us to enter the postseason without the passion and precision we'd exhibited all season long.

The September meeting highlights how you can address

your team to correct a troublesome trend. I called the meeting on September 16 in Tampa, after a 7–0 loss to the Devil Rays. That defeat was the capper of a 12–16 win-loss stretch, when we weren't playing with the same consistency that we had throughout the season. The fact that we'd gone flat did not upset me as much as what I'd seen in that 7–0 drubbing. We made fundamental mistakes on the basepaths, we made dumb plays in the field, we didn't run hard, and our bats had gone cold. Reliable hitters like Bernie Williams, Derek Jeter, and Chili Davis were mired in conspicuous slumps. We were lethargic—even sloppy—in most phases of the game. I was also rankled that two guys had arrived late to practice that day.

The game exemplified the worst of what I'd been seeing for a few weeks. The problems came to a head in Tampa, and I was undeniably ticked off.

I thought I knew the reasons for our lethargy. We'd already clinched our division, so we no longer had that incentive. Then there was the issue of breaking records. Going into August, we had won so many games that the major league record for most wins in a season—116—was within reach. So was the AL record of 111 victories. But I've never put much emphasis on breaking records, and I didn't think the team did, either. Yes, it was an exciting possibility. But our collective focus was getting to and winning the World Series. In any event, by early September, we'd racked up some losses and the record seemed more and more remote.

In Boston, just before the Tampa series, I had a chat with Paul O'Neill. "I can't put my finger on it," I said. "But the intensity just isn't there."

"I don't know what it is, Skip," said O'Neill. "I think guys are looking ahead to the playoffs."

I thought that Paul was probably right. There was little at stake in the short term, so guys were understandably thinking ahead. But they were asking for trouble. Sure, you can't maintain the same intensity level all season long. I wouldn't expect that. But what I saw in Tampa—the lazy play and lapse in fundamentals—is a virus that can infect a team. If you don't attack it fast, it can spread through a club like wildfire. Then the media seizes on the story of your losing ways, you get endless questions, and another virus—the one of negative thinking—starts to infiltrate from the outside.

If we continued to be doubly infected, we could have lost our edge going into the postseason. All season long we had intimidated other clubs, not with our arrogance but with our exceptional play. If our playoff rivals sensed fallibility in us, we'd have surrendered our psychological advantage when we needed it most.

Given what I'd witnessed on the field in Tampa Bay, I closed the clubhouse doors and let my anger show. As my players and coaches know, I usually accentuate the positive, so players were surprised by my tough tone and blunt language. "We stunk today," was my kickoff line. The room was absolutely quiet and still, though I did notice Bernie Williams sitting against a wall shaking his head.

I proceeded to identify players who'd made conspicuous blunders, including left fielder Chad Curtis, who threw to the wrong base on a bloop single in the fifth, allowing runners to advance. My purpose was not to single out anyone for blame; the whole team looked bad. Though I don't normally do this, I had to be specific about our mistakes because each was an example of what we were doing wrong. Chad made mental errors because he was trying to overcompensate for difficulties at the plate, but he and everyone else needed to recover their focus on playing sound baseball.

Then came the most impassioned part of my speech. "We've worked too hard, from February onward, to get where we are right now," I said. "Instead of daring others to beat us, we're beating ourselves." I emphasized that we had twelve regular season games left to straighten ourselves out before the playoffs. If we played lousy ball until then, we'd be setting ourselves up for a hard fall in October. I reminded them of just how well they'd played all year, then added a warning. "You can't just turn it off and on." My bottom line: Unless we recovered our focus, we'd be flirting with disaster. We could get wiped out in a five-game divisional series, and all our great accomplishments of '98 would be tarnished.

Everyone in the room paid close attention, which is exactly what I wanted. I didn't scream or yell, but the players understood how upset I was. David Cone and Paul O'Neill later said that I get angry so rarely that the meeting had a major impact on them. While I believed I'd gotten through to the team, I was still pretty pissed after the meeting. I felt sorry for my coaches, Don Zimmer and Jose Cardenal, who went out for a bite with me afterwards. I don't think I was very good company.

The next day we beat Tampa, 4–0. Hideki Irabu, one of the objects of my ire, tossed eight innings of shutout ball. In his previous five starts, he had had a 0–3 win-loss record and a bloated 13.30 ERA. The team played crisp defense and though we stranded too many runners, our bats came alive, with sixteen hits. We won our next game in Baltimore, and we ended the regular season on a hot streak, winning ten of our last twelve, including our last seven games in a row.

I can't overstate the importance of our final twelve games. Though it was too late to break the major league record for regular-season wins, we surpassed the American League record by winning 114 games. More important, we returned to form, regaining our concentration and confidence. Our pitching was sharp, and our defense was virtually flawless. Shane Spencer went wild, hitting those three grand slam homers in a span of ten games.

We entered the playoffs feeling good about ourselves again, with that cocky-but-not-arrogant attitude I'd seen all season long until early September. We won a remarkable eleven of thirteen postseason games, including four straight in the World Series, ensuring our legacy as one of the great teams in baseball history. If we had not recovered during the final regular-season games, which technically meant nothing in the standings and had no impact on postseason home-field advantage, I don't think we'd have ended our season in such a memorable, historic fashion.

The players get all the credit for responding to my challenges. If I'd been working with a bunch of guys who didn't care as much as these Yankees, they might have shrugged off my speech. But they listened hard, and they went out and played hard. The results speak for themselves.

Based on my experience, I recommend these guidelines for managers and executives as they plan and implement team meetings:

1. Use strategic team meetings when required, but don't overdo them.
2. Use meetings to address team performance or motivation sparingly.
3. Define your goals clearly so that your speech is focused and concise.
4. When necessary, allow yourself to display controlled emotion, since team players respond more readily to gut feelings than cold calculations.
5. Maintain your attitude of fairness, respect, and trust.

•   •   •

I have always believed in straight communication, both as a player and a manager, and it's as essential in the corporate world as it is in baseball. Whether you're an executive, manager, or team player, don't limit your definition of straight communication. It's not only about motivating people to peak performance. It's not only about reassuring employees of their worth to the organization. It's not only the best way to assure a proper flow of information within and between levels of the organizational hierarchy. And it's not only useful for lighting a fire beneath underachievers. Straight communication is all of these things, and more. Be as serious about mastering the art of communication as you are about every other phase of management, then observe the changes on your team. I guarantee you'll be surprised by the level of success your efforts will reap.

Torre's Winning Ways
Key #3: Straight Communication: The Key to Trust

- **Person-to-Person Guidelines**
  1. **Identify Individual Needs**
     - Determine what each team player needs, whether it's support, motivation, reassurance, or technical help.
     - Rely on positive messages to the greatest extent possible.
     - Remember that simple words of appreciation or insight can go a long way to motivate and focus team players.
     - Work to establish communication with team players from diverse ethnic and cultural backgrounds.
  2. **Time Your Talks**
     - Determine when the "door is open" for communication with a particular team player. Know when to nudge it open with helpful or directive comments.
  3. **Acknowledge Emotions**
     - Let team players know that you accept the range of their emotions, including fear, uncertainty, or anxiety.
     - Teach team players that they can't be courageous unless they acknowledge their own fears.

- Develop a balance between expressing emotions and keeping them private. Emotional control is appropriate on the field of work/play.

4. **Get Issues Out on the Table**
   - Air grievances and deal with problems in an open manner. You will prevent resentments that sap motivation and teamwork.
   - Bring these three qualities to your dialogue: clarity, honesty, and civility.
   - You can express anger effectively without resorting to screaming tantrums.

- **Use Team Talk to Ventilate and Motivate**
  - Use strategic team meetings whenever needed, but rely on motivational meetings sparingly.
  - Define your goals clearly so that your speech is focused and concise.
  - Display controlled emotion, since team players respond more readily to true feelings than cold calculations.
  - Maintain your attitude of fairness, respect, and trust.

CHAPTER 4 Key #4: Maintain Serenity (As Best You Can)

People say that I don't show much expression in the dugout, even in the late innings of nail-biting ball games. While I might seem to be calm in these situations, I assure you that I'm not. My stomach churns, and I chew on plum or peach pits or atomic bomb "red hots" to reduce stress and keep my mouth from getting too dry. When the game is on the line, I only appear to be stoical. Inside, I'm usually anxious as hell.

How can I admit such a thing in a chapter on serenity? I do so for a reason. People in baseball or business don't become more serene by pretending they aren't afraid. I argue the opposite: An individual under pressure is more able to be calm when he can admit he's as scared as the next guy. That doesn't mean he should publicly display his fear—just acknowledge it to himself and his close colleagues.

My coaches and players know that I get a little anxious during tight game situations, no more so than during the postseason. But I also don't make a show of my anxieties. I don't pace, I don't yell, I don't fidget very much. That's not my style. But my players know I'm human, and they know it's OK with me for them to admit their fears. At the same time, my steady demeanor lets my team know that I'm in charge, even when my stomach is in knots.

You can let employees know of your fears while retaining your steadiness. This combination reinforces trust and confidence.

I don't presume to tell other managers how to behave. Every executive has his own way of communicating and leading his or her team. But I do think that everyone, manager and employee alike, can benefit by developing their ability to remain calm in tough circumstances. You'll never be stress-free, but you can become more even-tempered and clear-minded under pressure, setting a good example for your team players. In this chapter, I present five specific guidelines for maintaining serenity (as best you can).

Maintaining serenity takes work. I've always had a pretty calm disposition, so I guess my ability to stay in control even when I'm tense inside is part of my personality. But it's also something I've learned. When I first came to New York to manage the Yankees, I decided to eliminate as many distractions as possible for my team. Who wasn't aware of all the past firestorms in the most famous franchise in sports? The controversies involving George Steinbrenner, Billy Martin, Reggie Jackson, or my predecessor, Buck Showalter, were only the most notorious examples. Every move the team makes, every internal squabble, is examined by the media with a microscope. I knew that my success would depend on my ability to handle potential controversies with as much balance as possible.

Every manager should have a clear-cut job description. But every job has aspects no one tells you about when you come aboard, and it's your responsibility to figure out what they are. As skipper of the Yankees, I not only had to be a strategist and motivator. I had to eliminate, or at least reduce, the distractions my players would face. Whether these distractions would come from upper management, the owner, or the media, I felt I should do everything I could to act as a buffer, preventing my players from losing their focus on baseball.

Over the past four years, being a buffer has been one of my main jobs, and it's helped my team to become a cohesive unit. The lesson is clear: Managers in every organization should write down the parts of their job description that no higher-up has laid down for them. They should take on any role, within reason, that helps their employees maintain their focus, serenity, and ability to function as members of the team.

As manager of the Yankees, I could never relieve all the pressure on my team. Pressure is built into baseball, just as it's built into most jobs in our competitive corporate culture. In my line of work, the pressure is particularly intense in a big-market club where you can't escape the media's attention. But I've done my best to relieve *excess tension* on my players from the press and the front office. As I'll detail in chapter 9, "Deference, Distance, and Dialogue: Striking the Balance," George Steinbrenner is devoted to winning, and I've always respected him as the team owner and my boss. But I needed to limit the distractions my players must deal with, and maintaining a mutually respectful relationship with George has made this possible.

In taking on this task, I decided that I wouldn't overreact to events in the media and the Yankee front office. Sometimes the best response is no response, or, if you must react, to stay even-tempered. In the New York sports world, a team controversy is an opportunity for a media free-for-all. I could avoid trouble for myself and my team by being careful not to react rashly to events or stories in the press.

My advice to managers: You can reduce tensions for your employees by maintaining your own serenity and control to the best of your ability. This, in turn, reduces outside pressures on your team, whether from other departments in the company, upper-management, clients, or the media. As a result, your employees will have the breathing room they need to achieve peak performance.

You may get rid of all unnecessary outside pressures, but your team members will still feel internal pressure to succeed and to win, as they should. In baseball, business, and life, there's no avoiding pressure. I often tell ballplayers that it's possible to be *intense but not tense*. It's a good standard for team players in any profession.

How can you help your employees relax and perform to the best of their ability when the heat is on? How can you accomplish this for yourself? Rather than telling a hitter or a pitcher to "just relax," you talk to him about his approach, offering suggestions for how he can solve a problem. Maybe you change the subject altogether. You apply common sense in both your manner and the solutions you offer, and by the time the conversation is over, he may actually *be* more relaxed.

It's also essential that *you* find ways to become more relaxed. I've developed five guidelines to help you to become more serene in your approach on the job, whether you're a manager, executive, or team member at any level of an organization.

The five guidelines to serenity in business and life are:

1. Focus on the Present.
2. Maintain Your Perspective.
3. Control What You Can, Let Go of the Rest.
4. Feel the Fear, Succeed Anyway.
5. Keep Your Cool.

When you work on all of these areas, you and the other members of your team will be more able to remain calm and centered—even when the pressure seems unbearable.

Focus on the Present

During my eight years as a player with the Braves, I was fortunate to hit behind baseball's all-time home run king, Hank Aaron. One day, Hank and I were talking about batting slumps when he made a comment that's stayed with me ever since: "Each at-bat is a new day."

No matter what our line of work, we all endure slumps. When we find ourselves in a rut, "Each at-bat is a new day" is a line worth remembering. I'd take it even further: We don't just have the opportunity to start fresh each day. We have the opportunity to start fresh each moment.

When we take this philosophy to heart, what we're really doing is focusing on the present. We can learn from past failures and mistakes, but we shouldn't get stuck there. We can keep future goals in mind, but we shouldn't get stuck there, either. The only way to reach our potential is to focus on what we must do now—this moment, this day—to perform effectively and to win.

In baseball, a hitter mired in a slump can belt a home run on any pitch. A team on a prolonged losing streak can always win that day's game. In business and life, the best way to overcome a pattern of failure or loss is to refocus on today. How can I achieve my goals in *this* meeting, with *this* client, in *this* moment? How can I prepare myself mentally and emotionally for the challenge I will encounter *today*? How can I change my approach to get the most of my talents right *now*?

We lose our instincts and our smarts when we get caught up in outside distractions, past blunders, or worries about the future. We can't do anything about five minutes ago, much less last week. (We can only learn from the past.) On the other hand, we function at peak levels of efficiency when we focus relentlessly on the present. With the Yankees, media stories threaten to divert my players' attention, which is why I work hard to deflect controversies from our clubhouse.

One controversy could have destroyed our chances to realize our World Series dream in 1998. It occurred in the second game of the American League Championship Series against the Cleveland Indians, our American League rivals who the year before had halted our drive to a second straight World Series victory. Game Two at Yankee Stadium was a tight pitching duel between David Cone and Charles Nagy. The score remained locked at 1–1 from the seventh through the twelfth inning. In the top of the twelfth, Cleveland's Jim Thome led off with a single against Jeff Nelson, and manager Mike Hargrove brought in Enrique Wilson to pinch-run for Thome.

Next up was third baseman Travis Fryman, who laid down a bunt toward first base. Tino Martinez charged the ball, scooped it up and threw toward our second baseman, Chuck Knoblauch, who was covering first. The ball hit Fryman squarely in the back as he was about to touch the bag, then bounced onto the infield dirt, rolling slowly toward the rim of the right field grass. Knoblauch began pointing at Fryman and yelling at home plate umpire Ted Hendry, arguing for an interference call. (Fryman did not stay within the 45-foot lane along the first base line, running on the infield grass in fair territory.) As Chuck continued to contest the non-call, he ignored the rolling baseball, and Wilson hustled around the bases. His teammates and the fans in Yankee Stadium were in an uproar, yelling at him to go after the ball. Chuck finally got the message, but Wilson had already stumbled toward the plate with the go-ahead run. He made a headfirst slide that easily beat Knoblauch's late throw.

We lost the game 4–1. I thought Knoblauch was right: Fryman had interfered with the play by running outside the 45-foot lane. But Chuck should have gone after the ball and prevented the run from scoring, then argued the call afterwards. Unfortunately, though, his mistake was so conspicuous and embarrassing that it touched off a furor in the press. One New York tabloid newspaper ran the headline BLAUCH HEAD. The TV sports shows replayed his blunder endlessly. The media said we were in trouble, and they basically put Chuck on notice that he'd be blamed for our downfall should we lose to the Indians in the ALCS.

Talk about pressure. Chuck had already been having a difficult series at the plate. Now he was being called a goat who could end up being held responsible for the demise of the Yankees' dream season.

How Chuck and the team dealt with this adversity would become a big factor in our postseason fortunes. Every player understands how painful it is to be defined by one mistake, and we all let Chuck know that we stood by him. His teammates closed ranks in a wall of support, and I think it helped him to handle the onslaught of criticism. Even George Steinbrenner took him aside and told him to keep his chin up. But Chuck probably didn't help himself after the game by defending his actions, saying that he wouldn't have done anything differently.

But when he later watched a videotape of the play, Chuck had a change of heart, realizing that he'd made a mistake. It was his decision alone to hold a meeting with the press in Cleveland before our next game. The night before, Chuck asked to speak with me. It was widely assumed that someone in the Yankee organization coached him on what to say at the press meeting. I know that I did not. "What do you think I should say to them?" he asked. "Just tell them the truth, tell them how you feel," I told him. He was clearly concerned about saying the wrong thing. "When you tell them the truth," I added, "you never have to worry that you won't remember what you said."

Chuck went out and took responsibility for his blunder. He apologized to me, his teammates, and the fans. "I screwed up that play," he said bluntly. I didn't think he needed to apologize. We all make mistakes, and it's always been my philosophy that we stick together as a team—perfect or imperfect, win or lose. But he made the correct decision to publicly admit his mistake, because he righted himself with the fans and the press and he was able to put the incident behind him.

Knoblauch's admissions, along with the support he received from the players and staff, enabled us to move ahead. He came out in Game Three and had a better night at the plate (2 for 3 with a walk and the only run scored) than any other Yankee, though we lost the game 6–1 and went behind in the series two games to one. We regained our footing in Game Four, and we ended up beating the Indians in six games. And Chuck's bat came alive during our World Series sweep of the Padres. The Knoblauch "incident" may long be remembered, but only as a minor and ultimately meaningless footnote in our drive to a championship.

Chuck said some things in his press meeting that sums up our philosophy. "Obviously, we don't want to fall behind by two games to this team," he said. "But our team is full of strength and great focus." When asked how he was living with that image of the botched play, he replied, "You can think about it all you want, but there's absolutely nothing you can do to go back and change it." Good advice for anyone who's made a costly mistake on the job.

By handling adversity in this way, Knoblauch and the

whole Yankee team kept their focus on the present, moment to moment, game to game. Even losing the next game did not deter us.

Each at-bat is a new day, but we give ourselves the best chance of success in any given "at-bat" by minimizing distractions. We must put past errors behind us by taking responsibility for them, seeking advice and support, and getting back to work. We must tune out the noise in our work environment, whether it comes from upper-management, petty quarrels, or media coverage. That's another reason why a cohesive team is so vital. When employees care about one another, they help one another ignore the distractions and concentrate on each day. Just as the Yankees did for Chuck Knoblauch. When a manager understands the importance of focusing on the present, he insulates his employees from external noise, and he doesn't dwell on yesterday's screwups. That's what I have tried to do as manager of the Yankees, and it's a lesson that any manager can apply successfully in any sector of the business world.

Maintain Your Perspective

When I first came to the St. Louis Cardinals, in 1969, I badly wanted to prove myself, especially since I'd been traded for Orlando Cepeda, who'd been such a fan favorite. It didn't help that I joined the team in mid-March, so my time at spring training was abbreviated. We opened the season at home and I promptly went 0 for 6. At one point during that game, Willie Stargell of the Pirates hit a bullet toward me at first base. When I got down on one knee to make the play, the ball hit me all over, then caromed into right field. An embarrassing moment, to say the least. The great Hall of Fame pitcher Bob Gibson called time out, then motioned for me to come to the mound. "Joe, any time Stargell hits a ball that hard, just get out of the way." It was exactly the hint of humor and support that I needed.

But my dry spell at the plate continued, and after the next game I was 0 for 9. I joked to the media, "If I don't get a hit by the All-Star break, I'm going home." The next day, I was at home in New York, since we were playing the Mets next, when I received a phone call from the Cardinals' general manager, Bing Devine. "Even if you don't get a hit by the All-Star break, we don't want you to quit," he said. The call was another show of support that helped me get past my slow start.

A sense of humor. The support of teammates. Knowledge of our abilities based on past performance. The realization that tomorrow is a chance to do better. These are all ways to maintain perspective when we confront a serious challenge, or when we're performing below expectations. They all make up the "big picture" viewpoint we need to keep our confidence high.

The phrase is easily tossed around, but what does "big picture" really mean? When we've had a bad day on the job, whether it's because we've lost a deal, a client, or a hoped for promotion, we remind ourselves of the good days, the deals we've made, the clients we've landed, the steps up the ladder we've taken. If our careers are just starting, we remind ourselves of just that—we're too young to expect such quick advancement. We must learn from our mistakes, but we must also put them in proper context. The baseball analogy works: Struggling batters and pitchers benefit by learning from their mistakes. But they suffer from mistakes when they become so overwhelmed by self-doubt that they can't stay focused enough to make useful changes in their approach. In business, managers and employees are more likely to learn from their mistakes when they don't beat themselves up over them.

We must constantly gain perspective on where we've been and where we're going, and use that awareness to build our self-esteem. For instance, success during the many months of the baseball season is often measured in small fragments—the home stand, the road trip, the short series against a tough rival. But this becomes a trap when teams or individuals berate themselves over a lousy five games. Losing streaks may be cause for concern, but not panic. In baseball, we're ultimately judged by 162 games, not 5. That makes our sport much closer to experience in the real world.

In the world of work, we shouldn't judge ourselves by last week's errors or lost opportunities. We need to pull back the movie camera and get a wide angle on our long-term development on the job. As part of that process, it's important to give ourselves credit for the ways in which we've grown and improved.

Those of us prone to negative thinking must recognize that this mindset is our biggest obstacle to progress. Yes, we can be afraid. Yes, we can be disappointed in ourselves. But if we don't maintain a realistic, positive perspective, our job performance will be impaired.

Managers can often help their workers hold on to that

positive perspective. Toward the end of the 1998 season, our pitcher Hideki Irabu got into a rut and there was talk in the media that he would soon be sent to the bullpen, and that he might not make our postseason roster. In early September, right after we clinched first-place in our division, Mel Stottlemyre and I called him into a meeting. He didn't appear focused on the mound, and he was getting only more frustrated. Mel and I wanted to better understand what was going on with him.

It took a little prodding, but through Irabu's interpreter we learned that he was putting intense pressure on himself, fearing that every outing could be his last as a starter. We realized how much the media stories had been getting to him. "Don't listen to those stories, because if I'm even thinking about putting you in the bullpen or anything else, you're going to hear it from me first," I said. "So just be yourself instead of worrying that the hammer is going to fall any minute."

The meeting seemed to put Irabu at ease, and we noticed improvements in his pitching during his last few starts—his stuff was back. He was more relaxed on the mound, and we kept him on our postseason roster, even though we didn't use him. But it was important for Hideki to stay with the team, and midway through the 1999 season he has clearly gained confidence on the mound.

You can't be responsible for someone else's mindset, but you can sometimes make it easier for your colleagues and employees to maintain their perspective. Irabu was struggling because he was living in fear, and there was something I could do to lessen that fear. Keep an eye out for workers who are stuck in a rut. Then see what you can do to figure out why, and to offer the kind of simple, supportive communication that can make a difference.

Another way to keep perspective on events at work is to retain your sense of humor. Paul O'Neill is the Yankees' most volatile player, though his anger is aimed almost entirely at himself. When he's mired in a batting slump, it's because he fights himself at the plate. But Paul's saving grace may be his humor, which is always at his own expense. My bench coach Don Zimmer has a running joke with O'Neill, who, like Zimmer, hails from Cincinnati. Paul will return to the dugout after a bad at-bat, and complain for the umpteenth time that he stinks to high heaven. "Listen, Paulie," Zim will say, "I can definitely get you a job laying bricks in Cincinnati." The line cracks them both up. It's become a running joke, so now when O'Neill comes back to the dugout, he'll just say to Zim, "I'm ready to go, just tell me when."

Control What You Can, Let Go of the Rest

I hold a point of view that's not too popular these days: Being great at your profession doesn't mean you're going to be a winner. This one's even less popular: Giving 100 percent doesn't guarantee a victory, either.

I've learned these lessons from my thirty-five years of experience as a ballplayer and a manager. It's nice to think that if you're talented, driven, and hardworking, you'll achieve all your goals, but that's not always the case. Ernie Banks was an all-time great ballplayer, but he never won a championship with the Chicago Cubs. I certainly believe that you can optimize your *chances* of winning, but triumph is never a mathematical certainty, for one simple reason: When it comes to winning, there are factors you can control and others you just can't.

As a ballplayer, I only had control over what I did; I had no control over the ability and execution of my opponents. (You may do your job well, but the opposition may do it a little better.) As a manager, I have done the best I could with the players I've had, and of course this always depended on things outside my control, like front office commitments and team budgets. Until I came to the Yankees, I'd never been in a World Series, and while there's no one to blame for that, I don't blame myself, either.

Reality check: You don't control all of the conditions that make it possible for you to be a winner.

In your professional life you should follow this: *Control what you can, let go of the rest.* Why does this philosophy lead to serenity? When you control what you can, you know you've done everything possible to succeed. That means hard work, total commitment, painstaking preparation, and squeezing every ounce of ability from yourself. When you let go of the rest, you stop torturing yourself over every defeat. (People in sports or business who assume they have absolute control over their professional lives will doubt their abilities the moment things don't work out as planned.) Take this approach, and you can feel good about your efforts at work, no matter the outcome.

Every time you experience a failure, ask yourself two sets of questions:

1. Did the failure involve some lapse of judgment, concentration, or hard work on my part? If so, how can I improve next time?
2. Did the failure involve a factor over which I have no control? If so, can I recognize this and quit blaming myself?

Use the first set of questions to take responsibility for mistakes and learn from them. Use the second set of questions to identify areas where you have no control, and to stop wrestling with yourself over them.

Let me illustrate with a partial list of things I *cannot* control as manager of the Yankees: how my players actually perform once they're on the field; what my players are paid; when or how severely my players are injured; what the media says about me or my players; what my boss, George Steinbrenner, says or does regarding the team.

Now here's what I *can* control: all strategic decisions during ball games; how I relate to and teach my players; how I utilize my coaches and support staff; how prepared I am for every ball game; how I speak to the media and react to their stories; how I relate to George Steinbrenner and others in our front office; how I react to what George says or does regarding the Yankees; my input regarding player personnel decisions, though I have no final say over those decisions.

I recommend that as an executive, manager, or employee, you create your own lists of factors you can control and ones you cannot. Pay close attention to the list and heed its lessons. If I tried to gain mastery over things I really can't influence, I'd get myself into big fights with the media, my boss, and my players. On the other hand, if I gave up mastery over things I *can* control, I'd be a poorly prepared manager who gave himself little chance for either success or victory.

Managers and executives who worry over decisions made at other levels of the organization set themselves up for trouble. I've known many young baseball managers who constantly complain about not having the players necessary to win. I always offer them the same advice: "You have one of the elite jobs in baseball, and there was no guarantee that you'd be handed the best group of players. If you get a chance to manage in the big leagues, whether the owner spends fifteen million or seventy million on salaries, you've got to make the best of your opportunity."

The same rule holds for employees who complain about their managers or the executives who supervise them. If you're doing work you love, or work you don't love but which is a stepping-stone to a greater goal, you can foul up your opportunity by getting stuck in frustration and anger at higher-ups. Whether they don't provide you with adequate resources or they treat you badly, you've got to return to the question, What can I control, and what can't I control? If you can use communication skills to get more resources, or to improve your relationship with a boss, great. If you can't, stop wasting emotional energy on this set of problems. I'll have much more to say on these issues in the chapters on "Dealing with Tough Bosses."

Of course, it's only human to get frustrated when your working conditions are less than ideal. When I first managed the St. Louis Cardinals, the ownership made promises about all the high-profile ballplayers they were going to acquire.

Over time, I kept hearing how the budget wouldn't allow for these acquisitions. I was upset, but I couldn't let my frustration show, since that would have sent a bad signal to my players. Had I complained, they would have assumed that I lacked confidence in them. Moreover, it's a negative mind-set—"This situation stinks and it's all *their* fault"—that's as infectious as a virus. Everyone starts to feel powerless.

My advice to managers and executives who are angered by their lack of resources and power, or upset by their relationship with higher-ups: Recognize your frustration. Do what you can to improve your conditions. Then let go of the rest. You need to remain positive, energetic, and committed to the job at hand. If you oversee a group of employees, you must send them positive signals about what you can accomplish as a team, despite the fact that you may be hampered by others within the corporate structure.

Close teamwork also helps us let go of factors we can't control. When we work to achieve team goals through cooperative effort, we're less likely to get caught up in other people's goals and expectations. (In baseball, we can't get consumed by what the media thinks we should be doing.) In the world of work, when we concern ourselves with the notions and expectations of others well outside our department—not our teammates or immediate supervisors—we stray from areas under our control.

My ideas about control and letting go aren't new, but few of us apply them as diligently as we can. I've learned the value of letting go in both baseball and in my personal life, which mirror each other in remarkable ways.

Just prior to spring training in 1999, I had my annual

physical checkup. Since my brother Rocco died of a heart attack, and my brother Frank had a serious heart attack in 1984, I have made certain to have a Thallium stress test every year. My 1999 test revealed that my heart was in better shape than the previous year, and my percentage of body fat had gone down. None of this surprised me, because I'd been working out more vigorously than in previous years. I thought I was the picture of health. But I was told that my PSA blood test—for prostate specific antigen—was elevated, a possible indication of prostate cancer. My cardiologist, Dr. Joseph Platania, recommended that I have it checked again when I went down to Tampa for the start of spring training. A high PSA can be caused by other factors, he explained, but I'd better be certain one way or the other.

Thus began a medical merry-go-round. I had to wait for the second set of test results, which showed the same elevation as the first. Then I had a prostate biopsy, followed by another period of waiting for results to confirm or rule out cancer. Once I found out it was cancer, I had to consult oncologists and make decisions about treatment. I eventually decided to have prostate surgery, and it was performed in mid March by Dr. William Catalona at Washington University in St. Louis. Then I waited for more test results to find out about my prognosis and treatment options.

The truth is, I was frightened each step of the way. Normally, I try to retain a positive attitude about any challenge, be it personal or professional. But as I waited to find out whether I had prostate cancer, whether I'd have surgery, whether the surgery was successful and so forth, I found it much easier to expect the worst. Apparently, it's a common experience among people with serious illness: Hanging on to hope is painful when you'll be devastated if the news is bad. When you expect bad news, you feel more prepared for it, and if the news is good, you're immensely relieved.

Here was a situation over which I had no control. There was nothing I could do to affect those test results or the success of surgery, other than picking the best surgeon. It was a time for letting go. I turned to my wife, Ali, my family, and friends for support. And I turned to prayer, though not so much to ask for a complete recovery. I mainly prayed for the strength to deal with whatever fate had in store.

Once the surgery was over, I was suddenly able to put on the boxing gloves. Before, I had little if any control over my health, but now it was time for rehabilitation. There was a lot I could do to recover my physical strength, to sustain an optimistic attitude, to eat healthfully and use nutrition to strengthen my immune system. None of these efforts could totally guarantee that the cancer would never return. But the surgery had been successful, the cancer was contained, and while my doctors said I might need further treatment, the overall outlook was good. I strongly believed that if I played my part, I could minimize the chances of recurrence.

Dealing with cancer is obviously more distressing than dealing with everyday pressures at work, no matter how demanding. But I used the same principle of control and letting go—recognizing how I could influence my recovery and how I could not. I tried to bring as much balance to this process as I could, though it was tough. During this period, the middle of the night was the worst time, when fear and uncertainty kept me from the solace of sleep.

But when I look back at the big picture, I recognize that I exercised control at a much earlier stage of the process. I took care of my health by getting regular checkups and having the PSA blood test. (Though my annual physical is a routine of the ball club, I'd taken it upon myself to get regular checks when I was a broadcaster in the mid to late 1980s.) Had I not been getting a yearly PSA test, I probably wouldn't have had symptoms or detectable cancer for several years. By that time, my doctors tell me, the cancer would have been much more advanced and difficult to eradicate. I'm now committed to spreading the news about early detection of prostate and other cancers, because early detection probably saved my life.

So take control wherever you can to increase your chances of success, but don't waste energy on aspects of work you can't influence. Keep your balance, and don't let your lack of control in certain areas destroy your faith in yourself, the rightness of your goals, or the value of hard work.

Feel the Fear, Succeed Anyway

I emphasize serenity, but be careful how you interpret this message. Some people think, "I can't relax, so I'll never succeed," or, "I'm nervous, so I'll freeze up under pressure." This can get pretty twisted, and I've seen players decide that their pitching or batting slumps will never end because they can't completely relax. That's not the right way to deal with tension.

In 1998, our players felt intense pressure going into the playoffs, because they'd broken the American League record with 114 wins and were being touted as one of the potentially great teams of all time. But we knew that all our regular season accomplishments would be dismissed if we failed to win the World Series. As a result, our hitters were a little tense. Also, the whole team was upset when Darryl Strawberry was diagnosed with colon cancer just after the start of our divisional series against Texas. We breezed through that series in three games, but only on the strength of our pitching; our hitters were still fighting themselves.

After our loss in Game Two of the ALCS against the Indians, the game in which Chuck Knoblauch argued the ump's call as the go-ahead run scored, we came face-to-face with the possibility of our World Series dream going up in smoke. Before Game Three in Cleveland, I held one of those rare team meetings and told my players: "We're not having fun. We need to start having fun again." Afterward, Paul O'Neill said to me: "Skip, it's not fun unless we win." "You're right," I replied.

Sounds like a Catch-22: You can't win unless you're having fun, but you can't have fun unless you're winning. But in the days that followed, I found out that you don't have to get caught in that trap.

We did lose Game Three of the Series, so we were down two games to one—the only really dangerous predicament we faced all season. But Game Four was the turnaround, in which El Duque Hernandez rose to the challenge and pitched shutout ball into the eighth inning, enabling us to beat the Indians 4–0. Our bats gradually came alive—just enough to help us win ball games—and we never lost another game in the postseason.

Did our tension miraculously disappear? Definitely not. Instead, I discovered that my players could play tense. They never lost their determination and focus. They didn't let their fear destroy their ability to be patient, to make adjustments, to play with passion. It takes a special group to accomplish this, and the 1998 Yankees were clearly a special group.

Yet I don't see why people in every walk of life, or in business, can't learn from their example. It's been said before: Talent-wise, there were no obvious superstars on the Yankees. However, in terms of determination, focus, teamwork, and belief in themselves, they were all superstars. You don't have to be a genius to get the most out of your ability, even when the demands on you seem overwhelming.

Of course, we are liable to make the most of our abilities when we work and play with as little fear as possible. The five guidelines in this chapter are geared to help you achieve a relaxed intensity, the best state of mind and body in which to perform. But don't use this philosophy against yourself. Don't try to rid yourself of every ounce of tension or fear. Recognize that you can be afraid, admit your fear, and still function at a high level of effectiveness. I agree with the message of the book by Dr. Susan Jeffers, *Feel the Fear and Do It Anyway*.

If you're constantly afraid, it helps to talk about it. In recent years, some of our players have spent time with sports psychologist Fran Pirozzolo, who's worked with the Yankee organization. I know other baseball teams have also used psychologists. It gives players a chance to talk out their anxieties, to deal with things going on in their personal lives that might be getting in their way. Talking to a psychologist helps these players compartmentalize their worries so they can get out on the field and focus on the present. They don't get rid of their fears, but they can set them aside when it's time to perform.

In every walk of life and business, people are starting to realize that it's OK to ask for help. It's a good thing, and I suggest that managers and employees encourage each other to get professional help when they need it. (Though they must do so constructively—and with sensitivity.) I know that several of my players have benefited, though I don't know who all of them are—that's confidential. If you always try to keep up that facade of fearlessness, you're going to put a lot of energy into something that's not very useful. You can free up that energy for your job by working out your fears with a counselor or psychologist.

Some forms of stress management, such as relaxation techniques, can also be helpful. Many of our Yankee players hold daily prayer sessions. Plus, I think that our togetherness as a team reduces our stress levels, because we know we have one another's support through the tough times.

Some players seem to be fearless. They go out in the most pressure-packed situations and get the job done without seeming to break a sweat. Either they have no fear or, more likely, they have found a way to master their fears. I think of El Duque Hernandez, who pitched that pivotal Game Four of the ALCS against the Indians. We were down two games to one, and floundering badly at the plate. El Duque took the mound with our playoff hopes on the line. All of our season-long accomplishments rested on his shoulders, and he hadn't pitched in fifteen days.

But El Duque didn't seem phased. Here was a man who

defected from Cuba in a leaky boat in shark-infested waters. He and several companions landed on a small, uninhabited island in the Bahamas, where they spent three or four days with little food or water before being picked up by the U.S. Coast Guard. Whether the details are totally accurate, there's no question that Hernandez made a risky journey on the day after Christmas in 1997, and that he survived the ten-day ordeal with his body and spirit intact.

That same bravery must have helped Hernandez to handle the pressure of Game Four. I'll never forget the afternoon before the game, when I watched El Duque at brunch. Here we were, about to embark on a game of such magnitude, and he was smiling, serving people food, picking up their plates, laughing. I said to myself, "Wow, I don't know if we're going to win, but I know he's not going to be afraid."

He certainly didn't seem phased in the first inning. I was concerned about Hernandez getting into trouble in the early innings, since he hadn't pitched in two weeks. Right off the bat, Omar Vizquel singled and stole second, and then, with two outs, Manny Ramirez drew a walk. El Duque was having trouble locating his slider, and Jim Thome, who had hit two mammoth home runs in Game Three, was up next. On a full count, Hernandez tossed a changeup that Thome promptly launched into deep right field. As Paul O'Neill drifted back to the warning track, we all wondered if it was going out of the park. Paul made the grab right in front of the wall, and El Duque charged off the mound.

Unlike his journey from Cuba, the rest of the game was smooth sailing for El Duque. His command improved, and he had great success jamming left-handed hitters, which he'd had trouble doing in the regular season. With his high leg-kick, and his wide variety of pitches and arm angles, Hernandez had the Indians fooled for seven innings, giving up only three hits and no runs. Our 4–0 victory was undoubtedly the single most important win of our unforgettable season.

It was a gutsy performance, and I can't help but wonder whether El Duque was so calm and collected because, in the fear department, the ALCS was no match for a journey in shark-infested waters.

We all can benefit, I believe, by taking another view of our daily trials at work. If we get overwhelmed by fear, we should say to ourselves, "OK, this is scary, but compared to what?" Since my bout with prostate cancer, I have asked myself this question when I face challenges as a manager. Even when we can't calm down, we can always "feel the fear and do it anyway."

Keep Your Cool

There's no quick-and-easy formula for keeping your wits about you. But you can apply certain commonsense ground rules for keeping your cool. These are the ones I've used in my own baseball career:

1. Challenge people without raising your voice.
2. Practice patience in every endeavor.
3. Consistency yields calm: Don't let yourself get too low over one defeat or too high over one victory.
4. Resolve difficulties without resorting to threats or tantrums.

I've worked hard over the years to be patient with players, to not overreact to conflicts, dry spells, and losing streaks. I've hated loud noises and yelling since my childhood, so I prefer to work out problems in a peaceful way. When I was manager of the Cards, I once found myself intervening to stop a fight between first baseman Pedro Guerrero and reliever Todd Worrell. We had a rule that disallowed opposing players from our clubhouse, but Guerrero let in Sammy Sosa of the Chicago Cubs. Worrell, who is 6 feet, 5 inches, took offense and started the fight, which got ugly fast. I had to break it up, both verbally and physically, which was no easy task. People in conflict on the job should do everything they can to resolve arguments with dialogue instead of resorting to insults or screaming matches.

When controversy breaks out on the Yankees, as it frequently has in my three years, I've tried to remain the calm in the eye of the storm. I also preach that you can't let the highs and lows consume you, because you've got to play again the next day. In a 162-game schedule, ballplayers can't afford the luxury of feeling sorry for themselves or patting themselves on the back.

Life is a 365-day schedule, and the same wisdom holds in family and business. If we get too giddy over a triumph, we're going to fall hard as soon we suffer a setback. By maintaining an even keel, we can be more effective—calmer, smarter, more focused—in everything we do.

Patience is essential. I let my players work out of their slumps and pitching problems. The late Birdie Tebbetts, my manager with the Braves, once said of himself, "I'm tougher to deal with when we're winning than when we're losing." I'm the same way. I don't get on my players when they're struggling, because straightforward counsel will do more good. When we're winning, I can be a bit tougher, because I don't want them getting complacent.

I've learned a lot about patience since my diagnosis of prostate cancer. I had to stay out of the dugout for two months, waiting to get well and watching my team on TV or from George Steinbrenner's box. I often felt impatient about getting back to work. This reminds me of a funny moment last year with my daughter, Andrea Rae, which I related to the *New York Times* sports columnist Dave Anderson. She had been acting her age, which was two and a half, and my wife, Ali, kept telling her, "Andrea, I've lost my patience with you, I've lost my patience with you." A few minutes later, Andrea walked over to Ali and said, "Mommy, I've found your patience."

We can all find our patience, if we look hard enough.

Torre's Winning Ways
Key #4: Maintain Serenity

- Maintain an even keel, without pretending you're not afraid or tense when you are.

- Reduce tension on team players by maintaining your own serenity, as best you can, and by reducing or eliminating distractions.

- Follow these five guidelines:
  1. **Focus on the Present**
     - Each "at-bat," no matter your profession, is a new day.

- Tune out external distractions, whether from other departments, upper management not involved in your supervision, or the media.
- Put past mistakes behind you; avoid worrying about future obstacles.

2. **Maintain Your Perspective**
   - Don't overreact to current troubles; remember past accomplishments that help keep your confidence high. For instance: After a bad day, remind yourself of the deals made, clients landed, steps up the ladder taken.
   - Learn from mistakes; don't use them to beat up on yourself.
   - Hold onto your sense of humor.

3. **Control What You Can, Let Go of the Rest**
   - Recognize that getting the most of your ability is the only way to succeed, but it doesn't guarantee victory.
   - List those areas in your job where you have control, and those where you do not. Pay close attention, so that you do everything you can to seize control when possible, and let go in areas where control is not possible.
   - Don't worry about decisions or the exercise of power at other levels of your organization, unless you're certain you can make a direct and helpful impact.
   - Keep your balance; don't let lack of control in certain aspects of your work destroy your faith in

yourself, the rightness of your goals, or the value of hard work.

4. Feel the Fear, Succeed Anyway

- Recognize that you can be tense or afraid and still function effectively. Don't let your efforts to relax and stay calm turn into another way to hammer yourself—that will only cause you to tighten up more.

- If you're constantly afraid, it helps to talk about it. If the problems are largely personal, consider speaking with a counselor or psychologist. If they are strictly professional, talk to your manager or the upper-level executive who supervises your work.

- When stuck in fear, say to yourself, "OK, this is scary, but compared to what?"

5. Keep Your Cool

- Challenge people without raising your voice.
- Practice patience in every endeavor.
- Consistency yields calm; don't let yourself get too low over each defeat or too high over each victory.
- Resolve difficulties without resorting to threats or tantrums.

CHAPTER 5 Key #5: Sustain Optimism (Even During Slumps)

Drive. **Competitiveness. Determination.** Commitment. These are the qualities we associate with winners. But each one of these characteristics depends on one other: optimism. Without optimism—that gut-level belief that we can succeed—we are far less likely to realize our dreams. Setbacks and slumps will stop us cold if we don't have basic faith in ourselves. No matter how badly we want to succeed, if we don't feel optimistic about our abilities and our potential, every day is going to be a struggle.

Life deals its blows to each one of us. Whether the setbacks occur in our personal or professional lives, they can ruin our dreams for success—if we let them. Optimism is the ability to accept negative events without allowing them to destroy our resolve. I've learned many lessons about life from baseball, and here's an important one: It's not always going to be wonderful. Slumps are inevitable, they aren't signs that we don't have what it takes to succeed. Here's my bottom line: Acknowledge that you've had a bad day, but don't live there. Move on with as much confidence as you can muster.

If I hadn't followed this advice, I might have quit baseball a long time ago. I played ball for sixteen years, and every season, I dreamed about making it to the World Series. I didn't get there with the Braves, and when I was traded to the Cardinals in 1969, I thought I'd finally have my chance. The Cards had just made two straight World Series appearances. It was the first season of divisional play, and the only question in my mind was which Western Division team we'd face in the playoffs. What happened? We slipped to fourth place in the division that year.

It gets worse. My former club, the Braves, won the western division title instead. Their opponent in the National League Championship Series? The Mets, the team I was almost traded to instead of the Cardinals. The Mets clinched their eastern division title by beating us at Shea Stadium. Of course, I made the last two outs on a groundball double play. The Mets went on to win the World Series, and were dubbed the "Miracle Mets." I began to wonder if I was jinxed, and it didn't help that some of my teammates joked about my bad luck. Bob Gibson would say, "You know, we used to win before you got here."

Despite that shaky start, I had my best years as a player with the Cardinals in the early 1970s, including 1971, when I won the National League Most Valuable Player Award. But the Cards never made it to the postseason, let alone the World Series. I did, however, come painfully close on two occasions. In August of 1973, we were in first place in the eastern division with a four-game lead over the Mets. But

Bob Gibson tore ligaments in his knee and pitched only one game the rest of the season, which certainly hurt our chances. The Mets passed us in the standings and won the division by a game and a half.

The next year, 1974, we went down to the wire with the Pirates, who we trailed by one game on the last day of the season. Our final game against the Montreal Expos was rained out, so we waited for the outcome of the Pirates' contest with the Cubs. If the Pirates lost, we'd get an opportunity to beat the Expos in a makeup game, to be followed by a one-game playoff against Pittsburgh. It was not to be. The Pirates beat the Cubs, and the dreary trip home from Montreal was a low point in my baseball career.

In my years as a manager, only once did I come close to the World Series, which had become my own impossible dream. In 1982, when I was managing the Atlanta Braves, we ended the season one game ahead of the Dodgers in the western division standings. But we were beaten in three straight games in our National League Championship Series against the Cardinals.

I was immensely fortunate to have been hired as manager for all three teams I had played for: the Mets, Braves, and Cardinals. Yet I had some bitter experiences, in which I not only endured losing seasons but also front-office politics that undermined my ability to do the best possible job. After I was fired by the Cardinals in 1995, I thought that my career, and certainly my World Series hopes, had come to a crashing halt. Soon afterward, I was contacted by my good friend Arthur Richman, who was then working as a senior advisor to George Steinbrenner.

"Joe, would you be interested in managing the Yankees?" he asked. "Sure, I would," I told him.

Yankee manager Buck Showalter was on his way out, and I was on the short list of replacements presented by Richman to Steinbrenner. George called me at home and said, "You're my man." We talked for fifteen minutes, and my decision was made. On my way to Tampa to meet with George and his staff, I called my brother Frank from the airplane. "You don't need this crap anymore," he said, referring to all the past trouble I'd had as a manager. "But it's too good an opportunity to get to the World Series," I said. Once he heard the excitement in my voice, Frank gave me his support.

Had I been a pessimist, I might have looked back on my career and thought, "It's time to give up my dream." Or I might have looked ahead to a future working for George Steinbrenner in the so-called Bronx Zoo and said, "Thanks, but no thanks."

But I'm basically an optimist. I couldn't pass up another chance to make it to October. Rather than seeing this as one last, inevitable slide into disappointment, I saw it as a solid opportunity with a talented team and an owner, no matter his reputation, committed to winning. I put the frustration and bitterness of the past behind me so I could give this new job my best shot. If I hadn't taken a positive view, I either would have turned down the offer or approached my new position with a lousy attitude. I certainly wouldn't have two World Series rings in my possession to show for it.

Optimism is more than just a glass-half-full view of events. I have found three specific ways to sustain a positive approach in our professional lives:

Key #5: Sustain Optimism (Even During Slumps)

1. Build Faith in Yourself
2. Find Refuge from Personal Troubles
3. Believe in Your Own Resilience

When you follow these guidelines for sustaining optimism, which I describe in this chapter, you won't stop having slumps or setbacks. But you'll be able to stop the vicious cycle in which defeats lead only to more defeats because your confidence gets shot. Managers who sustain optimism set a good example for team members, while optimistic team members are more effective in every aspect of their work. They have a stronger commitment to team goals, and they're more willing to work hard because they believe they can win.

Optimism is as important when you're on a winning streak as when you're on a losing one. While you need optimism to break out of a slump, you also need optimism to keep yourself from getting tight when success creates super-high expectations. The 1998 Yankees had to deal with these expectations as we entered the postseason. And the 1999 Yankees have had to play in the shadow of the remarkable achievements of the previous year. These situations have tested our confidence in ourselves, and we've had to rise to the occasion.

The 1998 Yankees in particular were an optimistic group who proved what is possible when an entire team, to a man, has such strong faith in itself. I've described our players as having an inner conceit. They never flaunted their pride or showed up other players or teams. I've always disliked displays of arrogance in sports, as when football players spike the ball or home-run hitters round the bases slowly to draw attention to themselves. I'm proud of my players' dignified and professional style of play. Most of the 1998 Yankees were really quite shy, but their inner conceit served them well as they rewrote the baseball history books.

These Yankees, as well as the 1996 and 1997 teams, were able to sustain optimism because they had a basic faith in themselves, they kept personal troubles off the field of play, and they believed in their own resilience. As a manager, I try to exemplify and teach these same qualities, since I know they are the basis for confidence in baseball, business, and life.

Build Faith in Yourself

Managers and employees alike must work to build faith in themselves, but they also can help one another with words of confidence and support. It's a simple philosophy, but one I've tried to practice in every phase of my career. From my playing days I remember how any expression of confidence from a manager, coach, or teammate—an upbeat comment or just a pat on the butt—made me feel a lot more comfortable when I was stuck in a slump.

I don't know many ballplayers so totally self-confident that they never need to build faith in themselves. Yes, the 1998 Yankees had an inner conceit, but each player still had slumps and the self-doubt that creeps in during those stretches. Are there any exceptions in baseball? Reggie Jackson doesn't seem to have any self-doubt, or at least any he'll admit to. Derek Jeter never stops believing in himself, though like everyone else he gets frustrated when he's not playing up to his own high standards.

Let's face it, self-doubt is part of human nature. We can't necessarily wipe it out, but we can build an enduring faith in ourselves that gets us through the rough patches.

Few of us are superstars. We have our gifts, but none so golden that we can be placed into that lofty realm. We should hold ourselves to the highest standards, but these standards should be appropriate to who *we* are. In order to build faith in ourselves, we must have a realistic sense of our talents, not an inflated one. If a career .250 hitter feels he ought to win the batting title, he's setting himself up for a blow to his confidence. If, however, he strives to hit .300, he's created a realistic goal, and if he adds 10 or 20 points to his average the effort will have been worth it.

Our faith in ourselves should be based on the knowledge that we're giving total effort to achieve realistic goals. Consider this commonsense comparison. You have two kids in school, you love them both, and they both work hard and do their homework. You see both children putting their nose to the grindstone every night. One child brings home a report card with straight A's, the other brings home a report card full of C's. What are you going to do, berate your child because he's a C student? He's not a failure; the C's are simply the best he can do right now.

Likewise, managers must consider the "skill sets" and personal strengths of their employees when they evaluate performance. If the person is working hard to get the most of his ability, the best thing you can do is offer support, whether or not he's setting the world on fire.

Employees must evaluate *themselves* by the same standards. Ask yourself: Am I doing my best to get the most out

of my abilities? When you answer yes, you have every reason to have faith in yourself and be proud of your accomplishments—whatever they may be. When you answer no,
you can renew your work ethic—the best first step to rebuild-
ing your self-esteem.

One way to build faith is to remind yourself of your capabilities. When you're full of doubt about whether you can
reach a goal or meet the standards set by your supervisors,
start thinking about best-case scenarios rather than worst-
case ones. The easiest way to do this is to *focus on your highest
achievements in the past*. It's common sense: If you've accomplished something great a few times, it means you can probably do it again. You may not be able to hit a grand slam every
time the bases are loaded in a game situation, but if you've
done it once you know it's possible.

One of the best examples is Andy Pettitte's postseason
pitching record. As with every pitcher, Andy has had his
share of difficult stretches, and I keep reminding him of what
he accomplished in Game Five of the 1996 World Series. He
pitched 8⅓ innings of shutout ball and we won 1–0, putting
us one game away from our World Series championship. I
know Andy carries that memory with him, and uses it when
he faces a particularly tough challenge. I think it helped him
when he took the mound in the fourth game of the 1998
World Series against the Padres, after having gotten roughed
up by the Indians in the ALCS. (It was also a week after his
father's heart bypass operation.) Andy put on his game face,
and he outpitched one of the National League's best pitchers,
Kevin Brown, shutting the Padres down into the eighth

inning. We won 3–0, and Andy's clutch performance capped our four game sweep of San Diego.

I tell my players not to go out on the field with the attitude, "Oh, I hope we don't lose this game." I prefer them to think, "There are two teams out here, and one of us has to win. Why not us?" The 1998 Yankees adopted this attitude, and it influenced how they approached every aspect of the game. All of a sudden, they were daring people to beat them. (When it comes to post-season play, my '96 team players were confident underdogs. In '98, we were favored, which made winning tougher, and made it necessary for us to maintain our edge at all times.)

Have faith in yourselves as a team. It may sound simplistic, but when you're confronted with a tough problem or competitor in your business, you can drill yourself with the same attitude: "Why *shouldn't* I prevail? Someone has to!" Start daring people to beat you, and you're less likely to get beaten. You can benefit from an inner conceit, which is most effective when you keep it to yourself and don't let your attitude turn into arrogance.

Don't tell yourself what you cannot do. Let your competition do that. Managers and team players alike must corner the market on positive thoughts. Roger Clemens has that self assurance, which is why he's a good fit in our ball club. Roger is not only one of the best pitchers of our era, he's one of the most driven, most professional players I have come across. When he showed up at spring training, I let him know that I expected the same things from all of my players, and he'd be no different. He understood completely; I didn't have to say another word. I told Roger that I admired what he'd accomplished, and that he reminded me of my old Cardinal teammate, Hall of Famer Bob Gibson, who was both an overpowering pitcher and an extraordinary competitor.

Clemens is one of those guys who has an ironclad faith in himself. He knows how good he is, and he won't hesitate to tell you what he believes he can do on the mound. He's not bragging, he's just stating facts. Roger has fire in his belly, and the talent to turn that fire into blazing achievements.

But here's an important lesson for managers and employees in any business: You don't need to have a Clemens-like level of ability in order to achieve great things in your profession. A baseball case-in-point is my third baseman, Scott Brosius.

After the 1997 season, we lost both our third basemen, Wade Boggs and Charlie Hayes. We had a promising young minor-league prospect, Mike Lowell, but we needed a stop-gap guy to play third until Lowell was ready to play full-time in the majors. The Oakland Athletics contacted our general manager, Brian Cashman, about trading Brosius to the Yankees. But Cashman had little interest—until he checked with Ron Brand, our West Coast scout. Brand was convinced that Brosius, then thirty-one years old, could make a contribution—despite a dismal 1997 season in which he batted .203 with 11 home runs and just 41 RBIs. (Scott had hit .304 with 22 homers in 1996, so it looked as though his career was on the decline.) We acquired Scott and signed him to a one-year contract. When he reported to spring training in 1998, I had no idea what to expect.

Key #5: Sustain Optimism (Even During Slumps)

It didn't take long for me to notice Scott's abilities, both as a fielder and a hitter. He had a strong spring training, and I wondered why he'd had such a bad year in 1997. As I got to know him, I realized that when Scott has a lull at the plate or a bad stretch at the "hot corner," as third base is known, it's because he tries too hard to fix things. You always hear how important it is to make adjustments in baseball. But a player can make so many adjustments that he loses sight of what he was doing right from the start. Scott and I talked about this problem, and I told him about my own experience with the Cardinals in 1972. After I led the league in hitting the year before, I went through one of those self-conscious periods. I started listening to too many people who had advice for me about hitting, and pretty soon I forgot what the hell it was I'd done to be so successful. When you're a nice person, you listen to people politely, and everyone has an answer for your ills. All of a sudden you find yourself at bat concentrating on everything but the pitch coming across the plate.

It was clear to me that Brosius had fallen into a similar trap in 1997. Once he got off to a good start in spring training, and fit in so well with our club, he began to perform on a much higher level than anyone had expected. He had another one of those self-conscious periods before the All-Star break, when he couldn't buy a hit and was struggling at third base. But he recovered his instincts and finished the year on a fielding and hitting tear.

How high did Scott soar? He hit .300 and drove in 98 runs during the regular season, a remarkably productive output for a hitter who usually batted eighth in our lineup. If that wasn't surprising enough, on a team of excellent hitters he was our best, most consistent batter in the postseason. Brosius hit a three-run homer to help us defeat the Indians in the final Game Six of the ALCS, but that was just a prelude. He practically handed us our Game Three victory against the Padres in the World Series by slamming two home runs. The next day, he singled home the third run of Game Four to help us wrap up our World Championship. It was only appropriate that Scott make the final out of the series. He jumped into the air, waving his arms in celebration, capturing the pure joy of the moment.

Scott's postseason statistics were mind-boggling. In thirteen games, the guy who many baseball people had seen as a journeyman batted .383 with 6 homers and 15 RBIs. In the four-game World Series, Scott hit .471 with 2 homers and 6 RBIs, more than enough to win him the Series' Most Valuable Player Award. Imagine how absurd it would have been to predict, at the start of the 1998 season, that the Yankees would sweep the World Series and that Scott Brosius would be the MVP.

Which makes Scott a perfect example of getting the most out of one's ability. Here was a third baseman widely thought to be in career decline—a guy in his early thirties coming off a terrible year—who joined the right team at the right time, worked hard, and showed just how good he could be. I'm sure Scott was reenergized by leaving a losing ball club and coming to a perennial contender like the Yankees. He added to our team spirit and was very receptive to our coaches and myself. Ultimately, though, it was Scott's determination, his belief that he could play to his potential, that enabled him to accomplish so much in 1998.

Scott Brosius didn't begin the 1999 season on the same level as 1998; he's had his ups and downs. But he knew from his 1998 experience how possible it is to rebound, and that knowledge will guide him for the rest of his baseball career.

No matter where you sit in the corporate hierarchy, you can learn from the Brosius example. His story illustrates that you can't base your self-esteem on your most recent downfall. Why tailor your expectations for yourself to the lowest common denominator? Do everything you can to create the best conditions for your own success, while staying optimistic that you can continue to learn and move forward. If you notice a decline in your productivity or creativity, don't fall prey to the idea that you're on a slide, and you'll never recover. That's the worst sort of self-fulfilling prophecy. Have faith that hard work and an optimistic attitude will enable you to get the most out of your ability. That's the best sort of self-fulfilling prophecy.

Find Refuge from Personal Troubles

It's hard enough to sustain optimism when you're faced with tough obstacles at work, whether they're external—a powerful opponent—or internal—your own self-doubts. When you add personal troubles to the equation, it becomes an even greater challenge, one that really tests your resolve. That's why we have to find a way to keep our personal problems from overwhelming us on the job.

I've had my best years in baseball as manager of the Yankees. During these same years, my brother Rocco died; my other brother Frank became seriously ill and underwent a heart transplant; and I was diagnosed with prostate cancer. It's been a tumultuous time, but as painful as these events have been, my work has helped me deal with them more effectively. I have learned how to put my personal difficulties in perspective, which has been one key to my ability to stay optimistic.

In late June of the 1996 season, we played a Friday double header against the Cleveland Indians. George Steinbrenner had made no secret of his desire for us to win both games in his hometown. In the first game, we fell behind 5–1 before rallying to defeat the Indians 8–7 in ten innings. We had a two-hour break between games, and I went back to the visitor's clubhouse for dinner. Before the second game began, my wife, Ali, telephoned to tell me that my brother Rocco had died. He had been home with his wife, Rose, watching our game on television. Soon after seeing our comeback victory, he fell over and died instantly of a heart attack.

It was a terrible shock, especially because Rocco hadn't been ill. I told Ali that I needed to call Rose and take a few moments to decide what to do. When I called my wife back, I told her that I was going to stay with the team and return on Sunday. Rocco was gone, there was nothing I could do, and I had my responsibilities with the team. I left during the second inning of Sunday's game and flew home. I said good-bye to Rocco that night, and he was buried the next morning.

Rocco's death broke my heart. But I felt that the best way to handle the heartbreak was to focus my energies and attention on work. I had a special opportunity with the Yankees, and a special season was unfolding. In any event, Rocco would have wanted me to try to realize my dream. I owed it to him and myself to channel my emotions into my job. I saw baseball as a gift, a refuge from the pain of loss.

Four months later, when we won the American League Championship Series against the Baltimore Orioles, the floodgates opened. I was finally going to the World Series, and a tide of emotion washed over me. I thought about all the friends and family members who had stood by me, and I felt Rocco's presence. As my players celebrated on the field, I went into the clubhouse, where I hugged my wife and baby daughter. I broke down, and the tears of joy were mixed with tears of sadness over having lost Rocco, the older brother I loved and admired so much. Ali remarked that I hadn't had time to grieve during the season, and I think she was right. I had done what I felt was necessary to meet my responsibilities to the Yankees—and get to the World Series. Once I knew I'd made it, I let down my guard and felt the sadness I had pushed aside.

We all experience grief, loss, and other personal pressures that can distract us from our work, and we have to let those feelings sink in. But we all have our own timetables for grieving and recovery. Many people who suffer from loss or stress find refuge in work, perhaps because the pain is too hard to bear in the days that follow. Weeks or months later, it may be easier to deal with those emotions. At least, that's what happened to me in the aftermath of Rocco's death.

My brother Frank's heart transplant, coming on our day off before Game Six of the 1996 World Series, was another stressful event, though it had a happy ending. Here I was, one victory from a World Series Championship, when I got a phone call at six o'clock in the morning from Frank's friend Jerry Goldberg, who was at Columbia-Presbyterian Hospital. I was told that they had found a heart for Frank. We'd been waiting months for this news, hoping against hope that a suitable heart would turn up when Frank was at the top of the donor recipient list. A twenty-eight-year-old man from the Bronx, of all places, had died from brain disease, and his heart was available. The surgery would occur, I was told, within the hour.

We had just won three straight games in Atlanta after two losses at home, and we were returning to Yankee Stadium on an incredible high. We were about to complete one of the most improbable comeback victories in recent World Series history, and Frank was being wheeled in for heart transplant surgery. My emotions zig-zagged from fear to relief to joy. The fear came first, but then I realized how desperately we'd been waiting for this day to come. All I could do now was sit by the phone. Hours later, I got the call that the surgery had been successful, and Frank was in recovery doing beautifully. When I went to see him early that evening he couldn't speak but he did write me a note: "Nice going." I couldn't have known it then, but Frank would eventually recuperate and return to his old self in a matter of weeks, though, of course, he went through some predictably rough periods.

Despite being exhausted, I was so hyper from the events of the past two days that I slept only two hours that night. My focus had to return to baseball. Game Six was another cliffhanger that required me to make a number of strategic moves, especially in the sixth inning, when I used three pitchers to protect a 3–1 lead. Our closer, John Wetteland, gave us a scare in the ninth when he put the tying runs on base. With two outs, Marquis Grissom knocked in a run with a single to right field, and the Braves cut our lead to 3–2. One more hit and we'd lose our lead; one more out and we'd win the Series. I was so nervous that I could only sit on my hands. Mark Lemke, one of those hitters who always seems to deliver in postseason play, was up after Grissom. But Wetteland got him to pop out to Charlie Hayes in foul territory. Hayes grabbed the ball, and the moment I'd dreamed about for thirty-seven years had finally arrived.

The celebration was unforgettable. My coaches mauled me in the dugout, and when I freed myself from the pile I ran out on the field. I hugged my players, and joined their wild run around the edges of Yankee Stadium. It was a victory lap like no other, with Wade Boggs sitting astride a policeman's horse and all our guys screaming with joy.

Managing Game Six was the experience of a lifetime, but I'd had to keep my mind on baseball when my heart was with Frank. This strikes me as a good example for managers and employees who are struggling with personal difficulties—the illness or death of a family member, a child in trouble, an ongoing divorce. Baseball has always been a shelter for me when times got tough. Whether the problem has involved a loved one or my own physical health, I know that for several hours I can lose myself in the strategy, the gamesmanship, the ebb and flow of a ball game. The camaraderie of teammates also can be a great comfort. We shouldn't use work to avoid problems, but when we *are* working, I think it's healthy to lose ourselves in the pleasures and challenges of our daily tasks.

During my two-month recovery from prostate cancer

surgery, I didn't have baseball as a refuge, but I did have time for my wife and my three-and-a-half-year-old daughter, Andrea, who kept me hopping, happily, for weeks. I also watched our games on TV and spent evenings at the Stadium when the Yankees were home. Emotionally and physically, I had good and bad days, even good and bad hours. But I tried to deal with the aftermath of cancer surgery one day at a time.

It was a relief when I came back to work in May 1999. The dugout was my shelter from all the questions and distraction from the media, and I was doing what I most love to do. But my cancer diagnosis also prompted me to get my priorities straight, and fast. I realized that my health and family came first, my career second. It's not that I care less about baseball, but I have a stronger sense than ever before of its place in my life. If I don't win this game or this series or this championship, I'll be disappointed but not crushed. I'll never have any concern that is greater than my health or the well-being of my family members.

My advice to high-powered executives, managers, and employees: Don't wait to get sick to set your priorities straight. Value your health and your family and friends, because they aren't replaceable. There will always be another deal, client, market, or promotion around the corner. This approach is not only healthier, it will probably help you perform better on the job. Whether you're in sports or business, you can get awfully tight when you feel that your life is riding on every new development. Remind yourself that it's just a game, or a deal, or a promotion—not a medical test for a grave illness. You'll approach your work with much greater calm, equanimity, and optimism.

Believe in Your Own Resilience

Optimists are resilient because their faith in themselves is so strong that they never count themselves out. Bucking the odds, coming back from defeat—these qualities are not based solely on chance, though luck often plays its part. Teams with the ability to stage comebacks, whether during a pennant chase, a playoff series, or a single ball game, are usually made up of individuals who believe in their own resilience.

I know from experience. The Yankee teams I have managed, especially those of 1996 and 1998, have had that bounce-back ability. Sure, we had plenty of lucky breaks go our way in '98, like bloop singles, bad hops, and umpire calls in our favor. But we've also had players who made good things happen, and believed in their own resilience, who have so much confidence and poise that they never stop scratching and clawing to get a victory.

Managers, teams, and individual team members benefit by believing in their own resilience. In chapter 10, "Steadiness and Small Bites," I'll describe a strategy that works for both baseball and business that will help teams and team members become more resilient. But resilience is more than a method. It's an attitude we can draw upon as we confront any challenge, whether it's one we face today, this month, this year, or throughout our professional lives. Resilient baseball teams can strike at any time when they seem down and out in a ball game, a series, or a season. Resilient managers and employees are no different: They bounce back from adverse events, whether those events affect one deal or the whole arc of a career.

Our 1996 team was a textbook example of resilience. We staged comeback after comeback in our divisional series against Texas, in the American League Championship Series against Baltimore, and the World Series against the Atlanta Braves. As this pattern continued, we began to *expect* to win games in the late innings. The more we *saw* ourselves as resilient, the more resilient we became. It was one of those instances of mind over body: Believing that something is possible makes it possible.

I learned from these Yankee teams that having faith in our own resilience makes us more relaxed, confident, aggressive, instinctual—even smarter. By maintaining a positive atmosphere in the workplace, managers promote an attitude of resilience in their employees, and employees can develop their own resilience. It's just a state of mind, which is something we can certainly build upon. We can't change our personalities, and there's only so much we can do to change our bodies. We can always change our minds.

Derek Jeter is one of the most resilient players I've ever managed. It's obvious in the attitude he brings to every game. He never feels that we're going to lose, no matter how lopsided the score. Often, when we're trailing badly, I'll go to the mound to change pitchers and Derek will be there. "We're going to win this one," he'll say, and deep down, he believes it. I can't say enough good things about his mental approach to the game.

The greatest postseason comeback I've ever managed was Game Four of the 1996 World Series. It was another critical contest, since we were down two games to one, and a loss would have put us into a deep hole in the Series. I'll detail how we pulled off that one in chapter 10. But suffice it to say that by the fifth inning, Denny Neagle was throwing a two-hit shutout and we were down 6–0. No Yankee team had ever come back from such a large deficit in a World Series game. But we chipped away, scoring three in the sixth inning. In the eighth inning, we rallied again. With two men on base and one out, reliever Mark Wohlers threw a hanging slider to our catcher Jim Leyritz, who hammered the ball over the left-field fence. His three-run shot tied the game at six runs apiece. We scored the winning run in the tenth inning, when Braves' left-hander Steve Avery faced Wade Boggs with a full count and the bases loaded. Avery threw a fastball just high, and Boggs's walk scored Tim Raines from third. We held on to beat the Braves, 8–6, in one of the more memorable come-back games in World Series history.

Beating the Braves in the 1996 Series was an exercise in resilience. We were considered down and out after two lopsided losses at Yankee Stadium in Games One and Two. Most sportswriters and critics wrote us off, considering the track records of the Braves' brilliant starting pitchers and the fact that our next three games were at Atlanta's Fulton County Stadium. No one dreamed that we'd win three straight on their home field and return to Yankee Stadium to wrap up the series. No one except me, my coaches, and my players.

But resilience is something we can apply to long- as well as short-range goals. In 1997, we were beaten by the Indians in the divisional series, three games to two. It was a heart-breaking letdown for a team made up largely of the same players who had staged so many thrilling comebacks during their 1996 title run. Indeed, Game Five looked like yet another storybook win on the path to a championship. We were down 4–0, but with clutch hits by Bernie Williams and Wade Boggs, we cut their lead to 4–3. In the ninth, Paul O'Neill missed hitting the tying home run by a few feet, and Bernie Williams flied out to end the game.

Many of the players were stunned by our loss to Cleveland. The way the 1997 season ended, they were left with a feeling of emptiness. Put simply, we not only knew that we *could* have beaten them, we felt like we *should* have beaten them. Not to take anything away from Cleveland, an excellent team then and now. We just thought we were better.

But we turned our deep disappointment into something useful: dogged determination. During spring training of 1998, I sensed that my players were anxious to prove that we shouldn't be judged by that five-game series against the Indians. We wanted to show that our 1996 title was no fluke, that we were a championship-caliber team that could rise to the top again.

I had to reassure key players who felt they'd let themselves and their teammates down, including Mariano Rivera, who gave up the game-tying home run to Sandy Alomar in Game Four, and Bernie Williams, who made the last out of the series with the tying run on base. They hadn't let us down, they only faced the reality that we can't succeed every time out. I remember telling Bernie: "You have to let it make you stronger."

Most of our 1997 players remained with us in 1998, and they all seemed to get stronger from the Cleveland series. From the start of spring training, they demonstrated true resilience by working and playing to the best of their abilities. There were still slumps and setbacks that season, but the team always kept them in perpective. The results in 1998 speak for themselves.

Again, you must believe in your own resilience on a daily, monthly, and yearly basis. Businessmen and women who've had a bad year should consider how they can bounce back from any sort of setback. Here's my advice: Openly confront your disappointments, determine areas that need improvement, identify important goals you have yet to achieve. Decide that this is the year when you'll turn things around. Dwell on your strengths, not your weaknesses, as you move toward these goals. Learn from your past defeats, and let them make you stronger.

That's how I approached the Yankee job from the moment I was hired, a time when I was trying to rebound from painful setbacks in my professional life, including being fired by the Mets, Braves, and Cardinals. The previous Yankee manager, Buck Showalter, had just left the team, and many people were upset with George Steinbrenner for letting Showalter get away. He was a popular young manager who'd done a fine job developing a talented group of players. To say that the media wasn't thrilled when I took his place is an understatement. The day after I was introduced to the press, the headlines in one New York tabloid read CLUELESS JOE.

I let none of this bother me. I was back home in Cincinnati by the time these stories ran. One writer faxed me an article suggesting that George was still courting Showalter, even though I'd already signed a two-year contract. I doubted the story, but there was nothing I could do about all the speculation and criticism. It helped that I saw this as a bonus job. I never expected to be skipper of the Yankees, or any other team, for that matter. When the job came my way I was so thrilled, and so pleased that George was committed to winning at all costs, that I let the media stories roll off my back.

I had been so down after getting fired by the Cardinals that I could only take a positive view of this development in my career. I also felt that I'd grown and matured as a manager, and with a solid core of players and the promise of more to come, I approached my new job with more hope than fear. Let them say whatever they want, I thought. I can only do my job, and try to have a good time in the process. I never would have imagined just how much fun I was going to have.

Teams and individuals can learn the art of the comeback. The key, I have found, is a positive approach to your work. Here's a basic example: You're interviewing for jobs and you get turned down three times in a row. You have a choice in how you look at these setbacks. You can say, "That's three strikes and I'm out. I'll never get hired." Or, you can say, "That's three no's closer to a yes." The optimist views obstacles differently from the pessimist: He sees opportunity where others see defeat.

I believe that the negative events in my career have enabled me to really appreciate the great things that have happened, especially as manager of the Yankees. If only good things happened, the victories would hardly taste as sweet. On the heels of a bad event—a setback, failure, or disappointment—keep going, working, pushing. When the light suddenly shines through, you'll have great satisfaction and a much deeper appreciation of your work and its rewards.

Torre's Winning Ways
Key #5: Sustain Optimism (Even During Slumps)

- Slumps and setbacks are inevitable. What matters is how we respond to them.

- Team members can develop an optimistic approach. Managers who sustain optimism set a good example for the team.

- Optimism is as important when you're winning as when you're losing.

- **Build Faith in Yourself**
  - You might not eliminate self-doubt, but you can raise your own confidence levels, and you can show confidence in your teammates.
  - Your faith in yourself should be based on the knowledge that you're giving total effort to achieve realistic goals.
  - Focus on your highest achievements in the past, and draw on those memories.
  - Don't dwell on what you can't do.

- **Find Refuge from Personal Troubles**
    - Deal directly with personal troubles to the best of your ability; then allow your work to be a place of refuge.
    - Allow the challenges and pleasures of work to be a respite, though not an escape from grief or personal disappointment.
    - Set your priorities straight, so you have a proper perspective on events at work. They're never life-or-death.

- **Believe in Your Own Resilience**
    - Resilience is an attitude you can develop. Never count yourself out regarding any goal or dream you deeply desire.
    - Dwell on your strengths, not your weaknesses, as you proceed toward your goals.
    - Learn from past defeats, and let them make you stronger.

CHAPTER 6

Key #6: Trust Your Intuition (But Rely on Your Management Team)

The game of baseball offers a model for decision making, one that can be useful and inspiring to people in the corporate world. In fact, business managers can look to their baseball counterparts for real guidance. A baseball manager has to be mentally prepared. He has to know his opponent's strengths and weaknesses. He should have statistics on hand to help him decide about match-ups between particular pitchers and batters. But a baseball manager must also trust his instincts. He relies on intangibles: his sense of when to be aggressive and when to be conservative; his instinct, drawn from experience, about when to pull a starter from the game; his intuition about whether a hitter's bat is coming alive or going cold. Many baseball decisions are based on a mixture of smarts and instinct, and I believe this is also true in the business world.

When corporate managers make decisions, they too must have facts at their command. They must know their markets, have sales figures at the ready, be aware of profit margins, understand what shareholders or clients are demanding. But they must also rely on instincts, because facts are never enough. Sure, you can always put the variables into a computer, and it will spit back a decision. Would that decision always be right? I doubt it. We still have human managers in business and in baseball, and it's our job to use our gut feelings, including our sense about people, when we make any important decision.

In baseball as in business, we managers have to do our research. We must gather information. But when it comes time to make game decisions, my stat book often goes out the window. I frequently play hunches, and they've worked out regularly enough to remind me to trust my instincts. You can be sure that I'm not always right. But I'd be right less often if I went strictly by the book.

I made some unorthodox decisions in the 1998 World Series. In Game One, I played a rookie in left field, Ricky Ledee, rather than another rookie who'd had a great September, Shane Spencer, our recent hitting phenomenon; or Chad Curtis, an experienced hand; or Tim Raines, a reliable veteran. I'll explain my reasons shortly, but the decision was based on several factors, including a hunch. As it happened, Ricky came through brilliantly. But had my decision backfired, I would still have been comfortable with it. When you make moves based on sound reasons and gut instincts, you have no reason to second-guess yourself.

Managers need to be comfortable with their decisions, come what may. When you trust your gut and your intelligence, you should never second-guess yourself—unless you determine that you haven't adequately prepared. What makes managing in baseball and business so interesting is that you can't predict results with total certainty. It would be nice if managing were a perfect science. But if that were the case, there would be no challenge and no suspense.

However, one truth about managing is a hard fact. You've got to be able to rely on your management team. I'm fortunate to have a brilliant and supportive group of coaches, and without them I'd be much less effective in the dugout. For instance, my bench coach, Don Zimmer, and I constantly bat ideas back and forth. Zim gives me different perspectives, and he's a good litmus test for some of my gut calls. He also helps me to stay calm and focused, and his mischievous humor can always break the tense atmosphere of close ball games.

My three main guidelines for decision making, which I describe in this chapter, are as follows:

1. Combine Smarts and Instinct
2. Take Your Chances: Unorthodox Decisions
3. Rely on Your Management Team

Trusting your intuition—and relying on your management team—is sound advice up and down the corporate hierarchy. Decisions are made at every level by employees, managers, and executives. Wherever you stand on that ladder, you can optimize your effectiveness by doing your homework *and* listening to your gut—*and* relying on the best minds on your team.

Combine Smarts and Instinct

During the 1996 postseason, our team had an uncanny knack for come-from-behind victories. And I seemed to have a knack for making the right decisions. The media said I had the "Midas Touch," because every move I made seemed to work. I know that luck played its part in my good fortunes. So many plays went our way that I wondered if destiny was on our side. I figured we were meant to win the World Series when, in Game Three, Charlie Hayes topped a ground ball down the third-base line that was clearly heading foul. The ball rolled across the foul line before making a right-hand turn and landing in fair territory. Hayes was safe on first, and three batters later, Jim Leyritz tied the game with his historic home run.

Whatever the role of fate in our storybook '96 postseason, for the first time I was able to apply my managing principles on the grand stage of the World Series. It was incredibly challenging and fun, and when the '98 Yankees played so well, they gave me another shot. In the World Series, I relied as always on preparation, thoughtful strategy, and pure intuition. Here are a few examples, which I believe demonstrate an approach to decision making that anyone in business can apply.

I mentioned playing Ricky Ledee in left field in the first game of the World Series against San Diego. It was a controversial move, because I had three other options that people thought were more sensible. I could have played Shane Spencer, the rookie sensation who hit clutch home runs in both Games Two and Three of our divisional series against

Texas. I could have played Chad Curtis, a solid fielder who had proven his worth throughout the '97 and '98 seasons. I could have played Tim Raines, a seasoned team leader with playoff experience. Ledee, on the other hand, had only played forty-two games in 1998, his debut year. He spent most of the season with our Triple A team in Columbus, joining the team's postseason roster only after Darryl Strawberry was diagnosed with colon cancer.

Why, then, would I select Ledee? I had several reasons. First and foremost, he's a good defensive left fielder. So is Chad Curtis, but he's a right-handed batter, and we were facing a hard-throwing right-handed pitcher, Kevin Brown. I figured that Ledee, a left-handed hitter, might have better at-bats against Brown. Ricky is a low-ball hitter and Brown is a sinker-ball pitcher. I also considered the fact that Spencer, Curtis, and Raines had just gone a combined 2 for 24 in the ALCS against Cleveland. Finally, I factored in some intangibles. Ledee had only batted .241 in the regular season, and he went 0 for 5 in one appearance against the Indians. But he was hitting well in practice, and he was hungry for an opportunity to contribute. When I pieced all this together, I decided to put Ricky in the lineup.

Ledee made me look smart. In the bottom of the second inning, Chili Davis lined the ball off Kevin Brown's leg for an infield single. Brown then walked Tino Martinez and Jorge Posada, and with two outs, Ledee was the batter. Ricky laced the ball down the right-field line for a double, scoring Davis and Martinez to give us an early 2–0 lead.

It was a huge moment for our team and for Ricky. All we'd been hearing in the days leading up to the Series was that Kevin Brown was unhittable. Rickey's RBI double gave us an instant psychological boost, and put the Padres on notice that as far as we were concerned, Brown was not invincible. I'm sure the hit also relaxed Ricky, because he was in a groove for the rest of the game. He went 2 for 3 with a walk, reaching base in all four of his plate appearances, helping us to beat San Diego, 9–6. On the strength of his Game One performance, I played Ricky in left field in Games Two and Four, and he finished the Series batting a remarkable .600 (6 for 10) with 4 RBIs.

I'm not suggesting any perfect formula for decision making in baseball or business. The Ledee decision worked out, but it was nothing more than an educated guess. Which means that you combine hard information with your hunches to make the best possible call. In playing Ledee, I weighed all the reasons why he might be a better choice than the other three left fielders. But I also had to follow my hunch about Ricky's readiness for this assignment.

I have one goal with all my decisions: to do whatever is needed to win today's game. I'm loyal to my players, and I stick with people because consistency builds confidence. But if I feel I have to make a change in order to win, I'll do it. I don't ask players to like my decisions, only to accept that I'm doing my job with one thing in mind—winning. Whether I'm playing Shane Spencer or Chad Curtis or Ricky Ledee in left field, I'm using facts and intuition to give us the edge that day. My players understand that I'm human, that I can only make my best judgment, and that it won't always be right.

Every executive has to make tough calls when it comes to promotions and plum assignments. The first three keys—on knowing your players, trust, and communication—should guide these personnel decisions. If you create an atmosphere of trust, and you help people understand that you have the team's best interests at heart, they will accept your judgments. Let your team members know that they'll get their opportunity to make a valued contribution, even if it's not today.

When it comes to lineup decisions, I sometimes rely *more* on gut feelings than statistics. I look at body language, how players carry themselves in practice and in games. There are certain guys who love playing in the heat of battle, others who shy away from it. I can usually sense the difference. If a decision is a close call, I might use stats—such as a hitter's record against a particular pitcher—as a tie breaker. In other cases, I'll make a decision totally on the basis of feel, and I'll use statistics to justify it to the media.

Baseball and other sports require managers to make split-second decisions. You're usually judged by whether they work or not. But whatever your profession, you must realize that a bad result doesn't mean you've made a bad decision. I've made choices that turned out badly, yet I'd do the same thing over again. You should reassess decisions to find out whether you made a mistake in your calculus. If so, you can learn something that will prompt you to do it differently next time. But recognize that you can make the correct call and still not succeed, because some things are out of your control. If, for example, I pinch-hit Chili Davis with one out and the bases loaded, and he hits into a double play, it doesn't mean I made a wrong call.

During the 1997 regular season, I made a game decision

that caused me to second-guess myself. The score was tied in the ninth, and we had a rally going. The winning run was on third, and second baseman Luis Sojo was due up. The right-handed Sojo would face a right-handed pitcher, and I had to decide whether to pinch-hit Wade Boggs, a left-handed batter who makes good contact. I thought that the future Hall-of-Famer was the obvious choice. He struck out on three straight pitches and we lost the ball game.

In this case, I had not bothered to look at my statistics book to see how Sojo and Boggs had fared against this particular pitcher. After the lousy result, I checked the book and discovered that Sojo had had great success against this right-hander. I kicked myself for not looking at the book beforehand, thinking that I'd made the wrong call and it cost us the game. When I calmed down, I stopped beating myself up. I realized that I would have hit Boggs even if I had checked the book beforehand. Why? I didn't need a base hit with one out, I only needed a batter to make contact to score the go-ahead run. Boggs is a great contact hitter who rarely strikes out. While Sojo had better numbers, that would not have swayed my decision.

It's always a good idea to "check the book," meaning to gather all the facts at hand. But, as in the case of the Boggs decision, you might still let your instincts override the numbers. It's a matter of balance: If you repeatedly give more weight to feelings than to facts, and things keep turning out badly, you should pay more attention to hard information. If you always favor facts over instincts, and things keep turning out badly, you've got to start listening to your gut.

You never have to make excuses when you use a combination of smarts and instinct every time out, considering every variable and trusting your own good sense. When you take this approach, there's no reason to beat yourself up when a decision falls flat. It's a waste of energy to blame yourself, and it can be destructive to blame others. Make your call, accept the consequences, and move on. My bottom line: Sometimes it works, and sometimes it doesn't.

During the 1996 postseason, most of my decisions worked but a few of them were clunkers. As I prepared for the first game of our divisional series against the Texas Rangers, I had to decide whether to use Darryl Strawberry or Cecil "Big Daddy" Fielder as my designated hitter. Before our workout, Darryl came into my office and said, "Why don't you play Big Daddy, because I can handle not playing." He sensed that Cecil would have a tougher time if I kept him out of the lineup. I thanked Darryl, because he was letting me off the hook. But I told him that I was putting him in the lineup anyway.

My reasoning? Darryl had good statistics against the Texas starter, John Burkett, when both players were in the National League. They were old numbers, however, so I couldn't put too much weight on them. On the other hand, I sensed that Darryl was pumped for the postseason. He had postseason experience and the competitive fire I felt we needed from the outset. I was playing Darryl on a hunch.

My hunch did not work out. Burkett jammed our hitters with cut fastballs, and we made little headway at the plate. In a game we lost 6–2, Darryl went hitless in four at-bats. Darryl did contribute later in the postseason, so I had the right idea at the wrong time. Both Strawberry and Fielder came through with clutch hits that enabled us to win the title.

One of my hunches did pan out the very next day, in Game Two against Texas. It was a crucial game, because if we lost we'd have been down two games to none in the short five-game series. Pivotal is an overused word, but there was no doubt in my mind that Game Two was pivotal. I had to pull out all the stops to win.

By the third inning, we had fallen behind the Rangers, 4–1. Juan Gonzalez was a one-man wrecking crew, driving in all four runs with two homers. But by the eighth inning, we had tied the game at four runs apiece, and it stayed that way for four more innings. The game became a strategic dogfight. I had to use four pitchers to get three outs in the top half of the twelfth inning, which took twenty-four minutes. Then, in the bottom half of the twelfth, Derek Jeter opened the inning with a single. Tim Raines walked, and Charlie Hayes, my third baseman, came to the plate.

The night before, I had noticed that Texas third baseman Dean Palmer was having trouble throwing to first base. I decided that we should try to make him handle the ball whenever possible. I also remembered that when Charlie had joined our team in August, we were talking about sacrifice plays when he said, "I can bunt." Here was a good opportunity to test Palmer. I put on the bunt sign.

Hayes bunted straight down the third base line, and Palmer fielded the ball cleanly. But his throw was wildly off line, and it whistled past the first baseman. Jeter beat it home with the winning run. We tied the series at one game apiece, then won two more exciting come-from-behind ball games to win the divisional series.

The Palmer strategy had worked perfectly, but even here

we got an assist from fate. A light rain had begun to fall earlier in the game, and the ball may have been slippery. I give Palmer credit, because he was not playing at 100 percent, and he had to handle a wet ball. Yet we had to do whatever was necessary to win.

I've learned from examples like these that winning decisions—in baseball and business—are a mix of careful strategy, close observations, playing the odds, and pure intuition. Sometimes it works, and sometimes it doesn't. You've got to be a thinker, but at times you also have to be a gambler.

Facts and statistics should only be part of your calculations. I use scouting reports on opposing players, but I don't rely heavily on them. I don't overload my players with information, because I don't want them to lose their instincts on the mound or at the plate. Is there an analogy to business here? At first glance, no. We live in the Internet age, and we're constantly being told that information is power. But at the same time, I wonder if businessmen and women can also be deluged by too much information. Instinct counts as much in business as in sports, because clients, markets, competitors, and departments are all made up of human beings who make mistakes and are unpredictable. We can't underestimate the power of intangibles that no software or statistics are likely to tell us.

What are my employees' needs? What are my clients' needs? What gives my competitors a psychological edge? What gives *us* a psychological edge? What larger trends in society or the business world are shaping today's markets? I don't believe these questions can be answered by facts alone. Trust your intuition.

Take Your Chances: Unorthodox Decisions

While I never made it to the World Series before coming to the Yankees, I did post winning records in my first three seasons managing the Cardinals. George Kissell was my spring-training coordinator, an incredibly helpful advisor and friend. George paid close attention to our club's weak spots and he offered me sound advice on strategy. We also had a funny dialogue going. George would always ask, "Joe, who wrote the book?" On cue, I'd reply, "Nobody, George. Nobody wrote the book." It was George's way of reminding me that I could make any decision, no matter how unorthodox, as long as I had my own reasons.

Safe managing is not always good managing. If you manage to win, in baseball and life, you have to make some unorthodox decisions. Executives who constantly look over their shoulders—always wondering what higher-ups, people in other departments, or the media will say—are more concerned about popularity than winning. They should focus on doing whatever it takes to succeed, no matter how unconventional. Here in New York, the sports writers and talk show hosts are always second-guessing coaches and managers. I can't worry about what they'll say the next morning. My job is to win the game, not cover my ass.

In Game One of our 1998 divisional series against Texas, I gambled with two moves, both involving the same player. Once again, I had to make a tough decision about left field, the wild-card position ever since I came to the Yankees. Shane Spencer had hit .464 with 7 homers, 3 grand slams, and 20 RBIs over his last nine regular season games. By comparison, Chad Curtis had batted .149 in his previous 47 at-bats. But the Rangers had the highest batting average and the most hits in the league, so I wanted our best fielders in the lineup. Based on our run production all season long, I felt we had enough offense. I surprised a lot of people by deciding to play the solid-fielding Curtis in left, keeping Spencer and Tim Raines on the bench.

Game One was a pitchers' duel between David Wells and the Rangers' Todd Stottlemyre, son of my pitching coach, Mel Stottlemyre. With one out in the second inning, Stottlemyre walked Jorge Posada. Curtis then ripped a line shot past Juan Gonzalez into the right-field corner for a double, and Posada held up at third. Scott Brosius promptly singled to right, scoring Posada and giving us a 1–0 lead. When the next batter, Chuck Knoblauch, reached a two-strike count, I decided to take a chance.

I called for a double steal. The Rangers' catcher, Ivan Rodriguez, has a gun for an arm. I figured that if Brosius broke for second, Rodriguez would take the challenge and fire the ball to second base. Curtis would break for home on the pitch, with a good shot at scoring. But if Rodriguez held onto the ball, Chad would be a dead duck at the plate.

Knoblauch swung and missed, striking out. Brosius ran on the pitch, and as we predicted, Rodriguez threw to second base. Scott held up, getting himself caught in a rundown between first and second. This allowed Curtis to dash home, scoring easily before Scott was tagged out by first baseman Will Clark for the inning's third out. We went ahead 2–0, which was the game's final score.

The less risky choice would have been to let Knoblauch

hit without sending the runners, hoping he'd make contact and score Curtis from third. But I figured we were in for a low-scoring contest, and I would do whatever it took to scratch out an extra run. Given what I knew about Rodriguez, it seemed like a good gamble.

The double-steal strategy was risky but not reckless. That's how it should be whenever you make an unorthodox decision. You have to accept that you may look foolish if your move doesn't work. But if you know both your own team and your opponent, and you consider all the angles, your unorthodox moves stand the best chance of working.

One of my unusual moves during the '96 World Series made a lot of people cringe. In Game Five, southpaw Andy Pettitte was out-pitching the Braves' John Smoltz, with a four-hit shutout through eight innings, but a lead of only 1–0. Normally, with a lead in the ninth, I would bring out my right-handed reliever John Wetteland. But I wanted Pettitte to pitch to the first two Braves' batters in the ninth, Chipper Jones and Fred McGriff. Both Jones and McGriff were more dangerous against right-handers. Also, Pettitte had not even thrown a hundred pitches.

Leaving Pettitte in would be controversial, since Wetteland had been a dominant closer all year long. But that was just the half of it. With two outs in the top of the ninth, Mariano Duncan was on first base with Jim Leyritz at the plate. We were playing National League rules, and Pettitte was scheduled to bat next. I had hoped Andy would not come to the plate, because now I was confronted with a tough choice: Should I call on a pinch-hitter, hoping for an insurance run? Or should I let Andy hit, so I could keep him in the game to pitch the ninth?

Duncan stole second, and the Braves' pitcher, Mark Wohlers, proceeded to walk Leyritz intentionally. Wohlers's fourth ball got by the catcher and went to the backstop, enabling Duncan to move to third. My potential insurance run was ninety feet away, and Pettitte was due up. I could have pinch-hit Wade Boggs or Tim Raines, both good contact hitters. But I still wanted Andy to pitch, so I decided to let him bat.

Andy had a quality at-bat, but he flied out to end the inning. In the bottom of the ninth, Andy really put my decision to the test when he gave up a lead-off double to Jones. With the tying run on second and no outs, I stayed with Andy against the power-hitting McGriff. One more mistake, and the game would be tied—or worse. Pettitte got McGriff to ground out to the right side, while Jones moved to third on the play. It was time to bring on John Wetteland. As I described in chapter 1, "Big John" gave us a scare when he threw a pitch that Luis Polonia hit to the warning track in right-center field. Thankfully, Paul O'Neill snagged the ball for the final out.

If we hadn't preserved the win, I probably would have been run out of town for keeping Pettitte in the game. The result was far from perfect, but a win is a win, and I would make the same move today.

In any business endeavor, you've got to keep a laserlike focus on your goals. When you do, your tactics will be geared to success, not to pleasing people who aren't part of your team. Stop worrying about the critics and Monday-morning quarterbacks. If you keep thinking, "I don't want to fail" you're not thinking about how you can win. Be willing to take risks, and to stand up for your choices even when they don't pan out. When you rely on sound reasons and gut feelings to make decisions, you never have to fear the consequences of being bold.

Rely on Your Management Team

Executives and managers can hardly do their jobs without a smart and supportive management team. When these teams consist of the right people, the person at the helm is better informed, more relaxed, and has a stronger relationship with everyone in the organization. I know from experience, because I have a terrific management team with the Yankees.

When I arrived in 1996, two members of this team were already in place, bullpen coach Tony Cloninger and third-base coach Willie Randolph. I selected the rest, bench coach Don Zimmer, pitching coach Mel Stottlemyre, batting coach Chris Chambliss, and first-base coach Jose Cardenal. This unit has remained in place for the past four years, a testimonial to how cohesive and effective they are.

I have certain basic criteria for my coaches, and all of these men meet them to a T. I don't want coaches who just show up every day. I want coaches who like being where they are, who have some passion about their job. I need people around me who are upbeat. That's one of my biggest requirements. I need a great support system because the players need a great support system. It's the only way we can get our work done. And I want coaches who have their own opinions, not ones who are only trying to please me.

Think of a team as a large circle, and the management team as the core within. If that core is made up of people who don't enjoy their work, how can they motivate members of the larger team to play with heart and conviction? They can't. I do a better job, and my players maintain a positive attitude, because I have coaches who care about their work, enjoy what they do, and are committed to winning. These are good criteria for any executive as he or she selects a management team.

While I make final decisions about lineups and strategy, most of them are influenced by input from my management team. Mel gives me crucial information about my pitchers, and Chris does the same for my hitters. Tony keeps me apprised of how my relievers are throwing the ball. Because they do quality work, I'm able to make quality decisions.

I have a unique relationship with my bench coach, Don Zimmer, that I think is a good example of how executives and managers can rely on their management team. Zim sits next to me in the dugout, and typically, we discuss every option. Having him there is a huge plus, because so often managers are out on a limb by themselves. Zimmer's qualifications are ideal: He's been a manager himself four times, he's a gambler, and he's always honest with me. When I want to be creative, I know that Zim will take me seriously—he's often more willing to be unorthodox than I am. Given his knowledge and experience, Zim is like a security blanket—someone I can trust whenever I run ideas by him.

When we began together in 1996, it took a little while for Zimmer and I to get comfortable with our working relationship. When someone on your management team makes a suggestion that you don't take, you don't want that person to feel useless. At times it was difficult for me to say no to Zim for this very reason. But he kept reassuring me, saying, "Look, I'm going to give you a bunch of ideas. If you don't agree with them, that's fine." Soon, Don felt comfortable making suggestions and I felt comfortable when I didn't use them.

Of course, I take many of Zimmer's suggestions. We think alike, but we are far from mirror images of each other. When he was a manager, Zim was always taking chances— managing the way many of us would like to but don't dare. The gambler likes to send runners on full counts, call for the hit and run, try double steals and squeeze plays. Zimmer brings this aggressive approach to our exchanges, which keeps me on my toes. I kid with Zim that I'm still not going to hit-and-run with the bases loaded—one of the wilder strategies he tried as a manager.

While Zim comes from the aggressive school, his suggestions are always well thought out. In a regular season game during our first year together, we had men on first and second with Luis Sojo at the plate. The safe strategy was to have Sojo bunt, and I was prepared to give the bunt sign. But Zim turned to me and said, "Why don't you hit and run?" I said OK, and Sojo promptly doubled down the right-field line to score both runs. As far as I'm concerned, Zimmer's been a genius ever since.

I've learned a great deal from Don, especially in 1996,

my first postseason as a manager. During the regular season, I would pull my starting pitchers only when I thought it necessary, giving them leeway because they'd performed so well all season. Zimmer helped me realize that in the postseason, I couldn't afford that luxury. In Game One of our divisional series against the Rangers, Jimmy Key got in trouble early. Zimmer said, "You better get somebody up." I removed Key earlier than I would have in the regular season. In Game Four of the World Series, Kenny Rogers got shelled early on, and his body language worried me—he was pokey on the mound. We were down 4–0 when Kenny gave up two singles to start the third inning. Normally, I might have left him in to face another few batters. This time, I felt I had to pull him before we found ourselves in a blowout.

Any manager who has people like Zimmer on his team is lucky. Executives and management team members can develop relationships that have similar qualities: mutual respect, a willingness to listen, the comfort level to accept or reject recommendations, supportiveness, an upbeat attitude, and a decent sense of humor. Respect and support are especially important. Because he was a manager, Zimmer understands that you're out there on your own. Make certain that your team members appreciate the demands of your job. Likewise, be sure that you understand the demands of their jobs.

You don't have to be friends with members of your management team, but I'm fortunate to have friendships with my coaches. Zimmer introduced me to horse racing, and I introduced him to red wine. Now, when Don's at a restaurant with someone, he'll order red wine, swish it around in his glass, and start laughing. He'll say, "You know who taught me that, don't you?"

Zim's jokes cut the tension in what can be a very tense business. During the '96 playoffs, Cecil Fielder, a beefy power-hitter who looks pretty bad on the base paths, was on first base in a critical moment. Don turned to me and said, "OK, let's start the runner." This got a laugh out of me, relieving the pressure. We turned it into a "running joke," if you will. Players in the dugout started noticing how we bounced these lines off each other, and they'd start laughing. We began referring to each other as Goof One (me) and Goof Two (Zim).

After my prostate cancer surgery, my recuperation lasted from the middle of spring training until late May 1999. George Steinbrenner and I agreed that I should hand over the reins to Zimmer. I didn't want anyone else brought in, because I was concerned that it might disrupt the chemistry of our team. I stayed in touch with Zim and my staff, but I remained fairly hands-off, for two reasons. First, I was under doctor's orders to get as much rest as possible and to keep my stress level low. Second, I felt it was best for Don and the team if he didn't have to look over his shoulder.

It was hard for Zimmer at first, partly because he was suffering from severe knee pain. But I also think he wanted to tend the farm for me. Zim was very concerned about doing things right, and perhaps, doing things as I would. During this period, I told him, "Just be yourself. Manage as you would manage." Over time, Don developed his own comfort level, and despite his physical pain he did a great job filling in for me.

My time off for rehabilitation points to yet another reason

for having a top-flight management team. If something happens to you—an illness or family responsibility—you've got to rely on your team when you're unavailable. The approach I took with Zimmer works most of the time. Let the people you trust take over the reins, but don't expect them to mimic you. You picked them because you believe in them, not because they are yes-men or -women who can't function unless you're there to guide every move. When you demonstrate this trust, the relationships will be strengthened when you return.

Never underestimate the importance of your management team. You can't go it alone. If you think you can, you're asking for trouble. Pick people you respect and trust, and be willing to put your faith in them. Let your management team know that you value their opinions, even when you don't take their advice. Encourage them to share their views, no matter how different from your own. Disagreements on strategy, personnel, and tactics are healthy, as long as people can openly exchange their views. Remember, when your management team is strong, committed, and optimistic, the whole team benefits.

Torre's Winning Ways
Key #6: Trust Your Intuition (But Rely on Your Management Team)

- **Combine Smarts and Instincts**
  - Good decisions are a mixture of smarts based on information and hunches.
  - Recognize that you can make the correct call and still not succeed.

- You never have to make excuses when you've done your homework, and used your intelligence and intuition to make the best decision possible.
- Facts and statistics should be only part of your calculus. Rely also on your psychological understanding of your own team members and your competitors.

- **Take Your Chances: Unorthodox Decisions**
  - Safe managing is not always good managing. To succeed, you have to make some unorthodox decisions.
  - Consider choices that may be risky, but not reckless.
  - Accept that you may look foolish when unorthodox calls don't work out. When you rely on sound reasoning and gut hunches, you never have to fear the consequences of being bold.

- **Rely on Your Management Team**
  - You can hardly succeed without a smart and supportive management team.
  - Get people around you who are upbeat and passionate about their work.
  - Develop relationships with your management team based on a willingness to listen, a lively give-and-take, openness, trust, and a sense of humor.

CHAPTER 7

Key #7: Dealing with Tough Bosses I: Create Mutual Respect and Trust

A tough boss can block your path to success on the job. If you've ever had a difficult boss, or you have one now, you know what I mean. Every day you work hard to meet the challenges of your position, the hassles and the long-range obstacles to achievement. Yet your employer only makes life tougher. This boss may be the type who meddles in your business when he shouldn't. He may be so distant that he offers no guidance or support. Perhaps he's a screamer who's constantly on your case, making your work life a misery.

Whether your boss is too hands-on, too hands-off, or too quick to anger, you wish there was something you could do to deal with the situation more effectively. You feel you've lost your power, and you'd do anything to get it back.

I've had several tough bosses in my baseball career, and I've learned useful lessons about how to deal with them. For baseball fans, my most famous boss is my current one with the Yankees, owner George Steinbrenner. Most people view George as the ultimate tough boss. By reputation, he is intrusive, demanding, and dictatorial. Before I came to the Yankees, George had twenty-one different managers over his twenty-two years of ownership. Several of them were fired and rehired; Billy Martin was fired five different times. When I was hired in November of 1995 to manage in 1996, many people figured that my head would be on the chopping block soon after I stepped into the dugout.

But there's an irony here. Of all the bosses I've worked for in baseball, he's been the easiest. I have had a good, productive relationship with George ever since I came on as Yankee skipper. How is this possible? There are several reasons. George and I share a strong commitment—we are both intensely passionate about winning. Also, while no less enthusiastic, I think he has mellowed over the past two decades. George is demanding, but I don't think he's the same man who had nasty public feuds with Billy Martin, Reggie Jackson, and Dave Winfield. Also, after thirty-five years in baseball, I, too, have also matured as a person and a manager. Finally, I think that my approach to work relationships has helped us both. Some people have given me credit for changing George, getting him to mellow out. But I want to say up front that any credit for our positive working relationship should be shared by both of us.

The first key to dealing with a tough boss is to develop mutual respect and trust. I know it's a challenge with a boss who is difficult, but once you've decided to stick with a job, you have only one good choice—to try to make it work. Rather than feeling bitter and complaining, do your best to create an effective relationship.

I don't know whether it's a gift or a shortcoming, but

when I begin work for a new organization, I decide to trust the owner and the other members of the front office. I know that trust is supposed to be earned, but I think that we do ourselves a disservice if we don't approach every new position with total commitment. And commitment requires trust. We create a positive atmosphere when we give our employers the benefit of the doubt from the get-go.

"I hang pictures," is a phrase I've used whenever I start a new job. It comes from a conversation I once had with Ken Boyer. When I first managed the Mets in the late 1970s, Boyer, then the Cardinals' manager, visited me in my clubhouse office. Kenny noticed all the personal pictures I had hanging on the walls. "Wow," he exclaimed. "You expect to be here for a while?"

"When I start working somewhere, I just assume that I'm going to be there forever," I said. "It's the only way I can do my job."

It's not that I'm naïve. I know there is no guarantee that my managerial jobs will last, or that my trust in my employers will always be justified. To me, it's all about one's mindset. When I approach a situation with a positive attitude, it can create a ripple effect in the people around me.

When you put out trust and loyalty, you're more likely to get trust and loyalty in return. It's a rule that applies whether you're dealing with employees, your management team, or your boss. My philosophy has helped me to succeed with the Yankees and George Steinbrenner, and it's one that may benefit those of you with a tough boss. This chapter introduces my overall approach to dealing with tough bosses, and the two that follow offer detailed suggestions. To illustrate my philosophy, I'll mainly offer examples from my relationship with George Steinbrenner, though I will discuss my dealings with other team owners. Here, I lay the groundwork with two basic strategies:

1. Lay a Positive Foundation
2. Create Mutual Respect and Trust

You can begin with the following simple suggestions: Stop focusing on everything that's wrong with your boss. You can't change him, so don't waste energy bitching about him. You don't have to like your tough boss, but you do have to work with him. Recognize that when you take a job, it's best to accept the whole package. Decide that you *can* handle his demands, or his distance, or his anger. Don't allow your boss's negative side to bring out your negative side. Hold on to your serenity, optimism, and integrity, and you'll survive—even thrive—with the toughest boss.

I said as much when I testified to a U.S. Senate Committee back in June, 1999, appealing for more funds for prostate cancer research. "I'm a cancer survivor," I told the committee members. On a humorous note, I added, "I'm also a survivor of George Steinbrenner for four years."

Lay a Positive Foundation

In my first telephone conversation with George Steinbrenner about taking the Yankee job, he emphasized the importance of loyalty to himself and the Yankee organization. I assured George that this would never be a problem for me. I've always believed that you should be loyal to the person who hires you, if only because he's your boss and he pays your salary.

I had heard the stories of how George was too hands-on, George was intimidating, George was a bully. He was baseball's most notorious tough boss. I knew all about his past firings of managers and his volatile relationship with Billy Martin. None of this fazed me. After being fired three times myself, including from my most recent job as manager of the Cardinals, I was thrilled to have the opportunity. I hadn't expected to get another shot at managing, so I had the sense of freedom of someone with nothing to lose. I was ready to deal with the challenge of working for George, whatever that entailed.

Right away, though, I recognized the pluses of working for George. From the start, he made clear his commitment to winning. The Yankees already had a strong foundation, and George was willing to spend his money to get the best players available. He was giving me something I never had before: the horses to ride to the finish line. Having never been to the World Series in my three decades in baseball, that was worth everything. In my previous experience, upper management of both the Braves and the Cardinals never made good on their promises to get the best players available. Obviously, without quality players a manager is hamstrung. With the Cardinals, I often felt as though I were in a fistfight with a guy packing a pistol. We just couldn't compete on a level playing field. Based on what I knew about George's goals, and the early conversations we had, I trusted that he would stand by his promise to me, to put the best possible team on the field.

In my case, George made it easy for me to accentuate the positive side of working for him. Had I not focused on the upside, I would have had a harder time fending off reports about the downside. I'd known George on a social basis, mainly from cocktail parties and dinner functions sponsored by the Yankees or Mets. We'd hit it off well in those situations, but of course I knew that working for him would be a different story.

As soon as I was hired, I began hearing a chorus: "What are you going to do when George does this?" and "What are you going to do when George does that?" None of this concerned me, because George's desire to win mattered more to me than anything else. I was therefore willing to accept any difficulties that working for Steinbrenner would present. The whole package. This approach put me in the right frame of mind. I thought, when problems arise, I'll deal with them. I'll handle them because I have faith in my ability to do so, and because it's worth the effort—given George's commitment to winning.

After my first phone conversation with Steinbrenner about the Yankee job, I flew down to Tampa to negotiate my contract, then up to New York to meet with the press. I realized that George was in a bind, because the media had given him a hard time about Buck Showalter leaving. Right away, I saw that we both had a lot invested in each other. George and I negotiated my contract during the Tampa meeting with several of George's advisors and newly named general manager, Bob Watson. This time, however, there wasn't much to negotiate. He offered me a two-year contract for $1.05 million, the same money he offered Showalter. He wasn't going to budge from there, given the flack he was getting for losing his popular young manager. This was a small pay cut from my salary with the Cardinals, but I understood his position. As I had expected, George was a tough customer. But nothing he said or did made me regret my decision to move forward.

I joined the Yankees with my eyes wide open. But I made sure to keep them trained on the value of this job and the upside of working for George Steinbrenner. I could have spent time and energy worrying about what George was going to do, but all of it would have been wasted.

When you make the conscious decision to work for a boss, this approach can be your route to a productive relationship. Be aware of your boss's downside, but don't spend emotional energy worrying about what he *might* do that *might* cause you trouble. Put that energy to work to achieve your goals. If he does create problems, deal with them as they come, one problem at a time. Most importantly, keep your eyes on the prize—the larger goals you feel you can achieve working for your tough boss.

Create Mutual Respect

You can apply the keys to teamwork and strong relationships with your employees to your dealings with bosses and supervisors, namely: Know your employer, treat him with respect and decency, acknowledge but don't overemphasize his failings. Every team player or tough boss has his strong points and his flaws. Recognize that you can't have one side without the other. Bosses need to be trusted and treated with fairness as much as employees do.

Distinguish a boss who is cranky, nervous, interfering, or distant from a boss who is downright abusive. You can live with the former but not the latter. If your boss constantly humiliates you in front of others, treats you with disrespect behind your back, and undercuts your ability to do your work, you may decide you can't work with him. In my relationship with Steinbrenner, the good has easily outweighed the bad. It's always a trade-off. When the bad clearly outweighs the good, you can confront the problems in the hopes of solving them. If these efforts fall short, it's time to look for another job. In some circumstances, you may even have to leave the perfect position because your boss makes your life a living hell. But be clear about your choices: Don't let an unpleasant personality drive you out of a good job. You can cope with a tough boss, though not one who abuses you on a daily basis.

A key to making this relationship work is to create mutual respect with your tough employer. From the beginning, I let George know that as far as I am concerned, he's the boss. He's the owner, he pays my salary, he built the team. I don't begrudge him his status one bit. Likewise, from day one George understood that I run the team on the field. I determine the lineups and make the strategic decisions. I control what goes on in the clubhouse. I'll listen to his suggestions—yes, he does have suggestions—but the final call is always up to me. I've never gotten a mandate from George about what to do on the field. I don't expect I'll ever get one.

Our mutual respect was based on shared goals and an agreement about how we should treat each other. We've both lived up to that agreement, which is not to say that we've had no arguments. But to me, the fact that I could talk to George—that he made himself available—made it possible for us to develop mutual respect. When you have no opportunity to talk to your boss, it becomes damn near impossible to build trust. I liked both Ted Turner and August Busch III, but neither of them was very accessible.

After I was hired for the Yankee job, I took a second trip to Tampa with Bob Watson, who was the newly appointed general manager. I noticed that some people in the front office referred to George as Mr. Steinbrenner. Right from the start, I called him "George" or "Boss." I felt it was important for us to communicate on the same level. I'll return to this theme in chapter 8, but you can establish mutual respect and trust by approaching your boss on an eye-to-eye, person-to-person level.

It helped, too, that George understands baseball. When I came on as manager of the Cardinals, August Busch III had just taken the ownership reins from his father, Gussie Busch. Unlike Gussie, August had no love for baseball. He was a brilliant businessman, and I had meetings with him that I thoroughly enjoyed. He's a smart, vibrant personality who clearly does a great job running his business, Anheuser-Busch. But as owner of the Cardinals, he applied a mentality that was appropriate to the brewery business, not to the business of baseball. He didn't understand why you should give a player five million dollars a year, since that player could get hurt. I guess when you own a brewery, you figure that you can replace a broken piece of equipment but not a broken ballplayer, so why spend all that money. As a result, Busch never signed the players needed to turn the team into a serious postseason contender.

Also, I never had the open lines of communication with August that might have improved our working relationship. It was telling that my meetings with him were never one-on-one. He always had his associates with him. But ultimately, we didn't speak the same language. You can't change someone's mind if you can never get on the same wavelength. He was tuned into the bottom line, I was tuned into baseball.

If your boss is inaccessible, you should take whatever steps necessary to get a dialogue going. You may need to work up your courage to talk to your tough boss. What I said in chapter 4 applies here, too: Feel the fear, and do it anyway. Your success on the job may depend on whether you can create mutual respect and trust with your employer.

George Steinbrenner has called me up to discuss lineup decisions, which is strictly my territory. He's badgered me when we're slumping or falling behind in the postseason. But I can talk to him, and he cares so deeply about winning that I always understand where he's coming from. I enjoy being around George. He can be charming and generous in ways few people know about. I see how driven he is just by looking in his eyes. If he has ten minutes on his hands, it's obvious that he feels there's something he should be doing with those ten minutes. There's no question that George can be critical. If we're not winning consistently, or he thinks I've made a mistake, I'm going to hear from him. But I have never been hurt by any of his comments, for one primary reason. George can never be as hard on me as I am on myself.

I hope that people in the corporate world can take some inspiration from what I've learned working for Steinbrenner: namely, that George had been billed as the most stubborn, intolerable boss anyone could imagine. I can't comment on what George was like with previous managers. But with me his strong points—availability, drive, passion, and commitment—have been far more important than his flaws. The baseball owner believed to be every manager's nightmare turned out to be my dream.

There are some lessons you can draw from this. First, don't be frightened by a boss's reputation. Make up your own mind, and establish your own independent relationship with him. Second, you can create mutual respect and trust with bosses who are flat-out demanding. Third, maintain your balance and perspective in order to stay calm when the going gets rough. The same keys that apply to your relations with team players—straight communication, serenity, and optimism—apply to your relations with your supervisor. Finally, while you can't expect to change your tough boss, you can bring a positive attitude to the table, and there's a good chance he'll meet you halfway.

Torre's Winning Ways
Key #7: Dealing with Tough Bosses I:
Create Mutual Respect and Trust

- **When You Have a Tough Boss**
  - Approach your relationship with trust, even if it has not yet been earned.

- Stop focusing on everything that's wrong with your boss; identify his or her positive qualities.
- Decide that you *can* handle his or her demands, distance, or anger.

- **Lay a Positive Foundation**
  - Accept the "whole package"—both the positive and negative sides of your boss.
  - Deal with problems and conflicts head-on, one at a time, as they come.
  - Keep your eyes on the prize—the larger goals you feel you can accomplish with your tough boss.

- **Create Mutual Respect**
  - Treat your boss with the same respect and decency you want for yourself.
  - Distinguish a boss who is unpleasant from one who is downright abusive. You can deal with the former, not the latter.
  - Don't begrudge your boss his status or power.
  - Don't be frightened by your boss's reputation—establish your own relationship with him or her and bring a positive attitude to the table.

CHAPTER 8 **Key #8: Dealing with Tough Bosses II: Assert Your Agenda—and Your Integrity**

When you begin working for a boss—any boss—you establish certain ground rules for your job and your relationship. You find out what he or she expects from you, and together you define goals and strategies. You also make clear your agenda—how you plan to go about your business as you live up to your responsibilities. With good communication, you can get off to a running start. You've established the chain of command, your areas of responsibility, and what you expect to accomplish. In other words, you know where you stand with your boss.

Of course, communication is rarely perfect from the start, and some tough bosses don't make it any easier. But your business relationships are no different from any others—they need to be tended. You can always fix a misunderstanding or clarify an area of confusion. Think of these conversations as mid-course corrections. Your relationship with a boss really is like a marriage: Partners must be willing to change and grow to keep it healthy.

When you assert your agenda, you must pick your battles. Know when you have the right and the reasons to insist on something. With George Steinbrenner, it was understood from the start that I had authority in the clubhouse and on the field. I didn't have to fight him for that. When he makes lineup suggestions I listen and take him seriously. Sometimes I act on his advice, sometimes I don't. But we both know that those final decisions are up to me.

If I overreacted whenever George called with a suggestion, we would be arguing needlessly all the time. Because we know where we stand with each other, I don't get undone when George calls. I also know that George, working in tandem with our general manager, Brian Cashman, has final say over every decision about our roster. Just as I listen to his suggestions about on-field matters, he often listens to my opinions about players to keep, trade, or acquire. But I don't expect him to necessarily take my advice.

Leave your ego at home when you go to work; this is especially important when you work for an organization with a powerful boss. If I allowed my ego to get involved in my dealings with George Steinbrenner, I'd be butting heads with him every day. I would be allowing our strong partnership to go down the tubes, which obviously would benefit no one. When we've argued over decisions, our basic understanding has never been threatened.

In this chapter I offer three primary strategies for asserting your agenda, and your integrity:

1. Establish a Joint Agenda
2. Draw Lines in the Sand
3. Uphold Your Integrity

When you assert your agenda with your boss, be sure you know what's worth fighting for. Define areas of responsibility and power that are rightfully yours. Recognize that you deserve to be treated with dignity and respect. Hold on to your integrity at all costs. But don't let your ego take over. Let's face it, your boss has more power than you do. Once you accept that fact, your wounded pride won't get you in trouble.

Establish a Joint Agenda

Before you assert your own agenda, it's best to define the goals you and your boss share. What do you want to accomplish on this job? What dream or vision do you and your boss have in common? It can be anything—optimal profit margins, lucrative new clients, a big jump in market share, a public offering. Talk about this vision with your boss. Verbalize your shared goals, because it will immediately improve your working relationship.

Once you lay this groundwork, you strengthen your hand with your boss, whether he's tough or not. When you have powerful goals in common, he's more likely to accept that your methods may differ from his. When I began working with George Steinbrenner, I made sure he understood that our goal was the same—we both wanted a world championship. Sure, every manager wants a title. But George knew how badly I wanted a World Series ring—having invested thirty years of hard work toward that dream. And he badly wanted to believe that I would deliver.

When it comes to roster moves, George and I have not

always agreed. This is fine with me, because roster moves are his prerogative. When George suggests that I put a player in the lineup, bench someone, send a player to the minors, or put a pitcher in the rotation, I listen to his ideas. But I never make a move just because he told me to. Each of us has only one basis for these decisions—what's best for the team. George may agitate me when I don't take his advice, but this doesn't disrupt our relationship, because we have a basic understanding. He accepts my areas of authority, and I accept his.

For example, early in the 1996 season, George signed Darryl Strawberry from the independent Northern League, and sent him to our Triple A club in Columbus. I let George know that I wasn't in favor of Darryl joining our club. I hadn't heard many good things about him, but I had heard plenty about his past problems with alcohol, drugs, and the IRS. I also didn't think we needed Strawberry, since we had the veteran Tim Raines in left field. But George was insistent, and Darryl joined the team before the All-Star break.

The rest is history. Darryl brought energy, a good attitude, and home-run power to our 1996 ball club, making a major contribution to our championship season. He continued to contribute in 1997 and 1998, becoming a team leader who was looked up to by some of my younger players. Despite his current problems, Darryl has undeniably been a plus for our team.

Steinbrenner was also responsible for bringing outfielder Chad Curtis to our club. We got Chad in a 1997 trade for reliever David Weathers, who had pitched us out of trouble more than once in the '96 postseason. I resisted the move, mainly because I liked Weathers as a pitcher and a team player. But I had no leg to stand on, because David was struggling at the time. In retrospect, it was another good move, since Chad has been a positive addition in left field, and a valuable backup in center field for Bernie Williams.

Early in my career, I spent many sleepless nights trying to tell myself I was right after I had made a mistake. I don't know when it occurred, but at some point I had the revelation that it was easier to admit my errors. I learned that I don't have to be right, which has helped me sleep much better. I have made sure to let George know that he was right to sign Strawberry, and right to trade for Curtis, and to thank him for his good judgment.

The Strawberry and Curtis decisions demonstrate why you should stay open-minded about corporate moves you disagree with from the start. Whether you're an executive, manager, or worker, be willing to grant others the same credibility you want for yourself. When decisions pan out, don't begrudge the person responsible, or look for a way to undermine the positive result.

Having to be right is a trap. Your ego takes over, and you get yourself into pointless power trips with your boss or employees. You can also cut off your nose to spite your face.

Don't get me wrong—it's important to fight for what you believe in. But when you're really honest with yourself, you know the difference between a conflict that's all about your ego and one that's about your team's best interests.

I didn't have much to do with putting together the 1996 Yankee team—George Steinbrenner and Bob Watson were mainly responsible. But they did ask for my views in some cases. After I was hired, they debated whether to keep Mike Stanley, a good power-hitting catcher, or pick up Joe Girardi, a fine defensive catcher. I spoke with Mel Stottlemyre and Don Zimmer, who had coached Joe with the Cubs. We all agreed that Girardi would do an outstanding job handling our pitching staff. I have always looked for defense first in my catchers, so I lobbied in favor of Joe. George has always liked sluggers on his team, so he preferred Stanley, a popular player who was capable of hitting over twenty homers each season.

It wasn't easy getting George to allow us to trade for Girardi. Finally, despite his preference for Stanley, George agreed to the move. In 1996, Girardi did a great job stabilizing our pitching staff, and his defense was everything we hoped for. In our final Game Six of the World Series, Joe gave us an early lead with an RBI triple. He has established himself as a team leader who's been a great influence in our clubhouse. Joe's a highly intelligent young man who can write his own ticket in baseball management when he retires as a player.

Over the years, George and I have kidded each other about Girardi—he'll get on my case every time Joe makes an error. Recently, during my recovery from surgery, he asked me to join him in his skybox at Yankee Stadium. Girardi had just made a wild throw to third base on a steal attempt. This time, I beat George to the punch. "Boy, your catcher is having a horse shit day." Silence. He knew I'd taken the words right out of his mouth.

But it's a lighthearted jesting. During the recent off season, it was widely assumed that we would not re-sign Joe, since Jorge Posada was gradually taking over as our number-one catcher. Posada is a gifted young player with a lot of life in his bat. George could have saved money by letting Girardi go, but he felt strongly that we should bring him back. George has come to recognize how much Joe means to our club, for his defense, his leadership, and his mentor role for Posada. It speaks well of George that he set aside his need to be right when he kept Girardi. (This will surprise people who view George as totally stubborn and egocentric.)

While our styles could not be more different, George and I have established our joint agenda. We respect our differences, and there isn't much competitiveness between us. By privately giving ground, we both gain ground—for our common goal of winning.

Many of us are looking for more power on the job. We want to exercise control over our domain, whether it's an entire company or a department, agency, office—or sports team. Middle managers want to be in charge of the employees under their authority. Employees want the freedom to be creative in their work. When we feel that our boss or immediate supervisor is getting in our way, we get frustrated and angry, and we wonder how we can assert our agendas.

These examples from my relationship with my boss may be helpful. When you want to advance your own ideas and career goals, concentrate first on your shared agenda. A tough boss is not likely to listen if you just confront him or her with demands. However, if you get a dialogue going, and he sees that his interests and yours overlap, he's going to be more receptive. You generate good will, which goes a long way. Sometimes, that's all it takes for you to win the autonomy you've been seeking. In other cases, you have to keep working on the relationship. Your message should be that you have the interests of the company at heart, not just your own interests.

Your tough boss may never be ideal. But you can build a professional relationship that serves your needs, his needs, and the larger needs of the organization.

Draw Lines in the Sand

Your agenda, and your integrity, can sometimes be threatened by a tough boss who is unresponsive or undermining. That doesn't mean you should cut and run. In my view, you quit when all your best efforts to establish a professional relationship, one that allows you to work effectively, have failed. When you care about your job, it's worthwhile to make those efforts. Use straight communication to make your boss understand your concerns. When it comes to conflicts, the principle I've used with players also applies to bosses: *Deal with it.* Get problems out on the table so you can resolve them and get on with your work. Often, tough bosses will ease up when you have the courage to confront a problem head-on. As long as you do so in a dignified way.

You may ask: What if I can't resolve our conflicts? What if my boss still doesn't listen? What if he continues to make my work life impossible? It may be time to draw a line in the sand.

I've had to draw the line a few times in my career. One incident occurred with Ted Turner, the flamboyant founder of CNN and owner of the Altanta Braves. Ted hired me to manage his club in 1982. Initially, I was interviewed by the Braves' general manager, John Mullen. We agreed on a three-year contract with an attendance clause. (If the Braves drew more than two million people, I would get a bonus.) Soon thereafter, Mullen told me, "You were not my choice, but let's work together the best we can." I wasn't exactly thrilled by this greeting. I later found out Mullen had not told Turner about the attendance clause. Ted said he would never have agreed to the clause, so he dropped it from my contract. (I also made a mistake by not insisting on having the clause in writing.) My relationship with the Braves organization got off on the wrong foot.

None of this prevented me from doing my job. We had a terrific start, setting a major league record by winning our first thirteen games in a row. We spent the rest of the season on a roller coaster, with several losing and winning streaks, but we still won the western division, one game ahead of the Los Angeles Dodgers. Yet we lost the National League Championship Series in three games to the St. Louis Cardinals. I managed the Braves for two more seasons, and we finished second both years.

I liked Ted personally, but we never developed a sound professional relationship. Turner was actually more meddlesome than George Steinbrenner has ever been. During a game in 1983, we were trailing badly in the middle innings when I decided to pinch-hit some young players. I chose them over several veterans, whom I wanted to save in the event we got close. The next day, the press criticized the hell out of me for keeping my seasoned players on the bench. Ted asked to meet with me, and we spoke in a conference room adjacent to his office. Embarrassed and angry, Ted took the media's position that I had screwed up. He screamed at me furiously, right in front of a group of people from the Braves' front office. I felt humiliated.

We won the game that day, and Ted was in a good mood when he came into the clubhouse afterward. But I wasn't. I asked him to come into my office for a private conversation. I was fuming, and I let him know it.

"Ted, you're the owner and I respect you because of that," I said. "You can fire me or make any changes you want. If I worried about being second-guessed, we wouldn't have won last year. But don't you ever yell at me like that in front of other people. If you want to scream at me, fine. Just do it in private."

"OK, fine," he said. I think Ted got my drift. He didn't apologize, but he never dressed me down in front of anyone again.

Whatever my future with the Braves would be, I wanted the same respect I gave to others in the organization. You strengthen your self-esteem—your sense that you deserve to be treated as a professional—when you put a stop to that kind of mistreatment. I don't care whether you're a factory worker, secretary, middle manager or high-level executive. You should not have to lose your dignity in the workplace.

Turner and I never developed mutual trust in our relationship. It limited what we could accomplish, and it limited my tenure with the Braves. Organizational politics also contributed to my firing in 1984. But I did everything I could to make the best of an imperfect situation, which I think is essential for any professional. You can't always thrive in an organization. But you can always hold on to your integrity. In fact, when you survive a bad work situation with your integrity intact, you may even feel better about yourself.

With George Steinbrenner, I have never felt that my integrity was violated. We've had occasional conflicts in which we raise our voices, but they don't get us into trouble. We'll just get into a good-natured shouting match. When we negotiated my contract extension in 1998, we had our usual one-on-one encounter. We were yelling at each other when I stopped midway, and said, "We're not mad at each other, right?" "No, we're not," he said, and we finalized the deal.

In the late seventies, George and Billy Martin became infamous for their knock-down, drag-out verbal battles. Of course, I'm nothing like Billy Martin. More to the point, that was twenty years ago, and while George may still get irritable at times, we can talk things out.

Bosses and employers should be able to tolerate some good-natured quarreling. But you have to judge whether your employer has crossed the line. A boss should not humiliate you in front of others. He should not undercut your ability to do your job. He should be willing to listen to your opinions, even if he does not take them.

While you need to hold the line on these standards, don't be unrealistic. Every workplace has its share of bad-tempered executives and managers. There will always be people who meddle, backbite, and second-guess what you're trying to accomplish. You can usually deal with them. It's important, though, that you avoid pulling the same routines that you condemn in others. Treat your boss with respect even if he does not reciprocate. But draw the line when your dignity is at stake.

Uphold Your Integrity

Our most important asset as professionals is our integrity. Once we lose it, people are less likely to trust us. Our words carry little weight. Our actions become suspect. In dealing with a tough boss, or any group of higher-ups in your organization, you must do whatever it takes to uphold your integrity.

I had to wage some battles to maintain my integrity as manager of the St. Louis Cardinals. In July of 1994, the major league players walked out on strike. My relationship with the front office deteriorated during this period. The Cardinals' general manager was Dal Maxvill, my good friend and former teammate who'd been instrumental in my hiring. Just before the strike, Maxvill stood up for me at a meeting with August Busch in which I was told that my contract would not be extended. (It meant that I would go into the '95 season on the last year of my contract, something I had been promised would never happen.) Maxvill and Busch got into a screaming fight, and soon thereafter, Maxie got fired. My other key supporter, Stuart Meyer, the team president, retired. The guy who replaced Meyer, Mark Lamping, never even called me after he was hired.

To my surprise, I was not axed immediately. But I knew that Lamping and the newly hired GM, Walt Jocketty, were talking to other managerial candidates, so I figured that I was not long for the job.

The strike dragged on, and during the spring of '95, the baseball owners made plans to hire replacement players. I hated the whole idea, since I thought it was a sham to replace the best ballplayers in the world with a collection of novices and has-been players. I also thought the owners were crazy to believe that fans would buy into replacement ball. But I had signed a contract to manage the Cardinals, so I felt I had to meet my obligation.

During this spring training, August called a meeting with me and my staff. The theme of the meeting? How we could present a positive image to the press about replacement baseball. Beforehand, I asked to speak with August privately.

I pulled no punches with him. "Listen, I'll do anything else you want me to do," I said. "But I am not going to lie. I won't say that I'm in favor of replacements, that we don't need the regular players, or that I'm enjoying any of this."

But Busch was relentless. He continued to insist that I put a good face on this whole mess. "Look, the major league players are going to come back," I said. "If they see me quoted saying that we don't need them, how am I going to manage when they return?"

"How do you know they'll be back?" said Busch. "I have a pretty good feeling," I replied.

At that moment, I realized that we would never be on the same page. It was absurd to me that Busch and the rest of the owners seriously believed they could keep up this charade and call it Major League Baseball. A court injunction brought the players back in April—earlier than most people predicted. But my relationship with my Cardinal players was damaged, since they resented the fact that I had managed the replacement players, even if it was under duress. Our season began badly, and I was fired in mid-June.

To me, the argument with Busch was all about integrity. I simply refused to lie, to pretend that I was happy about something I considered a farce. If I had, I would have lost my credibility completely. When you lose that, you can no longer function well in a professional world where trust is—or should be—the currency of every exchange.

My managing career began in 1977 with the New York Mets. In 1980, Nelson Doubleday and Fred Wilpon bought the team, and they named Frank Cashen the general manager. Frank is a good friend today, but back then I was sure that I would not last long after his arrival, since owners and general managers want to hire their own people. During that year, Cashen sent Al Harazin, then his assistant GM, on road trips to oversee our club. Harazin observed every aspect of our day-to-day operations. Why did Cashen have Harazin on our case? Cashen was a stickler for organization, and he wanted to know what we were doing on an hour-by-hour basis. But I was also convinced, based on everything I knew, that he was rooting around for a reason to fire me.

I felt I had to confront Cashen with my suspicions. "Frank, if you want to make a change, make a change," I said. "I have no problem with that. But do me one favor. Don't look for a reason to fire me. Don't say we had to get rid of him for this or that reason."

I really harbored no bitterness about the prospect of being fired. I understood how baseball teams were run. I knew that Doubleday, Wilpon, and Cashen would want their own man. I also figured it was a miracle that I'd lasted five seasons in New York, considering my lopsided record of 286–420. But I was adamant that Cashen not come up with a fabricated reason to get rid of me. Again, my integrity was at stake and I had to protect it.

Cashen fired me on the last day of the 1981 season. Thankfully, he did not offer the media any specific excuse for letting me go. I left the Mets with my reputation intact, and with no ill will toward Frank or anyone else in the organization.

Don't go looking for these sorts of battles, but when your principles are on the line, don't shrink from them. Picking your fights is the simple prescription. In this regard, exercise good judgment by drawing on that combination of smarts and gut instincts.

Recognize that there may be little you can do about politics at higher levels of your organization. Within your own domain of power, you can usually exercise control over infighting and people whose egos are out of control. You can also shape your relationship with your boss or immediate supervisor, as I've shown. But rarely can you influence events and people on rungs above you in the corporate ladder.

I know this from experience. Organizational politics was a major factor in my firings as manager of both the Atlanta Braves and St. Louis Cardinals. In Atlanta, the fact that Ted Turner and I never developed a solid professional relationship was part of the problem. My record had been respectable—we won the division my first year and finished second in my next two years. But Ted had a group of baseball advisors who apparently had their own agenda. Before I was let go, I got wind of the fact that one particular individual had been pushing Ted to hire Eddie Haas, a man who'd been in the Braves' organization for years, as my replacement.

By the end of the 1984 season, it became obvious that I was on my way out. No one in the front office was returning my phone calls. Turner, who usually loved to burst into the clubhouse, was nowhere in sight. None of his deputies were showing up, either. The signs were not very subtle. I felt like I had a contagious disease.

The day after the season ended, I called for a meeting with Ted, fully expecting to be fired. Ted was rather uncomfortable when he broke the news. I told him what I believed— that a specific person in his organization had pushed for my release. "You're right," he said. But this individual had taken the same viewpoint as other baseball people in Ted's circle. I realized that I'd been an outsider from the start. They really wanted to promote from within.

Politics also played a part in my release from the Cardinals. August Busch was unwilling to spend money to get the players we needed to put a winning team on the field. In my view, he made a business miscalculation when it came to baseball. He wanted his team to deliver bottom-line profits the same way that the various arms of his beer business did. Other owners seemed more flexible, recognizing that it was unrealistic to expect their teams to be profitable at the same level as their other corporate entities. And most of them recognized what August did not: To optimize revenues from baseball, the least you can do is invest in a quality product. And that means players.

Though we posted winning records during my first three full seasons as Cardinal manager, we were never serious title contenders. Dal Maxvill, their general manager, was not only my supporter, but for almost a decade he had absorbed the blame for the failure of the organization to bring in quality players. As soon as people began to blame Anheuser-Busch, Dal was fired. August was not about to let his family business be embarrassed. The front office changed hands, my contract extension was never exercised, and it was just a matter of time before I, too, was fired.

When it comes to corporate politics, one of my guidelines in Key #4 is most important: Control what you can, let go of the rest. Be savvy about the politics in your organization. But don't let what you observe make you feel helpless. Do everything you can to control your own domain, no matter how small or vast.

When politics at higher levels threatens your job or integrity, get as much information as you can. Talk to your boss and your immediate supervisors. Be as honest and forthright as possible. Take action to defuse controversies and eliminate distractions. But know, too, that some organizational factors are beyond your control. When they make your work impossible, consider making a change. However, if you can accommodate yourself and get your job done, buckle down. Don't fall prey to helplessness and bitterness. Corporate politics are obviously a fact of life in the business world. Know the limits of what you can tolerate. But also know that you can still thrive in a tough work environment.

Torre's Winning Ways
Key #8: Dealing with Tough Bosses II:
Assert Your Agenda—and Your Integrity

- **Establish a Joint Agenda**
  - ◆ Openly discuss and define shared goals, the dreams or visions you both hold.
  - ◆ Set aside your ego. When you don't have to be right, you avoid unnecessary and destructive conflicts.
  - ◆ Concentrate on your joint agenda, then assert your own. Make sure your boss knows that you have the organization's interests at heart.
  - ◆ Fight for the principles and goals you believe in.

- **Draw Lines in the Sand**
  - ◆ Do not accept humiliation, harassment, or assaults on your dignity.

- **Uphold Your Integrity**
  - ◆ Defend your integrity, your most important asset as a professional.
  - ◆ Pick your battles carefully.
  - ◆ Recognize when politics at higher levels in your business are beyond your control.
  - ◆ When politics are at play, don't become helpless or bitter. Be proactive when possible, knowing that you can often thrive in a tough work environment.

CHAPTER 9

Key #9: Dealing with Tough Bosses III: Deference, Distance, and Dialogue: Striking the Balance

To sustain a professional relationship with a tough boss, it's best to stay calm, rational, and cool under fire. Sure, you may raise your voice once in a while. It might happen when you draw a line in the sand, defending your integrity. But for the most part, self-control is your best asset. Hold on to the mutual respect and trust you have worked so hard to build. Don't let your shared goals go down the tubes because you feel you must always be right.

You may ask: What if my boss pushes my buttons every day? How can I stay so calm and rational? With my experience with tough bosses in baseball, I've come up with an answer, and broken it down into four parts:

1. Show appropriate *deference* to your employer.
2. Use *distance* as a strategy—don't overreact to every event or dispute.
3. Generate an open *dialogue*.

4. Strike a *balance* among deference, distance, and
    dialogue. It's a formula that works.

The combination of deference, distance, and dialogue
has been effective for me with George Steinbrenner, but it
hasn't always succeeded throughout my managing career.
With Braves' owner Ted Turner and Cards' owner August
Busch III, problems arose in the areas of distance and dialogue. Namely, there was too much distance and too little
dialogue. I showed deference to them, but I was not given
much opportunity to communicate with either man. Without
dialogue, there isn't much you can accomplish with your
boss, tough or otherwise.

Your employer may be moody, egotistical, or belligerent.
But as long as he or she is accessible, you can use deference,
distance, and dialogue to cultivate a workable relationship.
You may even find yourself reaching heights of achievement
with a boss whom you never expected to be your partner in
success. I know, because it happened to me.

Display Deference

Showing deference to your boss does not mean being submissive. To me it means that you're loyal and respectful. You'd
be amazed how much you can accomplish with a tough boss
when you grant him that basic regard. At least in many cases.
You don't necessarily have to have breakfast, lunch, and dinner with your employer; nor do you have to believe in everything he stands for. But you do owe him your allegiance.

I took this tack with George Steinbrenner from the

moment I was hired, and we reached a comfort level right away. I'm sure it helped that I openly let him know he had my loyalty and respect. I came in thinking, no matter how the media depicts George, he's still a person. Every employee wants that basic understanding, and so does every boss.

This approach helped me to stay objective about George— I wasn't caught up in all the hype and fear about "The Boss." I realized there was no reason for me to take any of George's stuff personally. I saw him as an intensely driven person who tries to drive other people. A man with an insatiable thirst for success, but also a human being with a great deal of concern for others. (He does exceptional charity work that few people know about.)

George and I have also agreed not to run to the press with dirty laundry. One problem with daily sports coverage is that writers and broadcasters scoop up a negative comment, and it's rarely the whole story. Small sound bites get back to the people involved, and all of a sudden you have a real conflict on your hands. So if I have any grievances with George, I make sure to air them privately rather than make a grandstand play.

This is another sign of deference. Respect your employer's desire to keep problems between you. If you broadcast your frustrations, whether to others in your organization or to the media, it shows a kind of disrespect for both your employer and your job.

Deferring to your employer may seem outdated, but strip away the idea of being submissive, and it's not the least bit old-fashioned. The fact that you demonstrate respect doesn't mean you are less than equal. I don't see George, or any of my other bosses, as superior people because they have status, money, or power. Still, there is nothing demeaning about following your boss's directions. You can show respect without disrespecting yourself.

Use Distance as a Strategy

Some tough bosses are intimidating, intrusive, and rude. Others are detached and critical. Whatever your boss's traits, maintaining some distance is a good way to keep yourself calm and sane in the workplace.

Let me explain what I mean by distance. Since you need dialogue with your boss—more on that in a moment—you shouldn't remain so distant from him that you don't communicate. However, if you have an intrusive boss, you can often prevent him from getting overly involved in your business. Let's say you're a middle manager with your own staff. Your goal should be to protect your team from your boss's distractions. When you have established a good foundation for your professional relationship, you can assert your agenda—in this case, more freedom to manage your team as you see fit. (See chapter 8, "Assert Your Agenda—and Your Integrity.")

Distance also means not getting overly caught up in your boss's reactions. I don't care if he rants and raves. Don't let petty disputes or sideshows destroy your focus on the work at hand. Do not become so emotionally involved in pleasing or battling your boss that you take your eyes off that prize.

You need constructive criticism, so be open to your boss's comments. But it's important that you distinguish between criticism and insults. The insults can hurt like hell. If your boss belittles you, take a step back. Remind yourself that it's his problem, not yours.

Distance can be a psychological approach. I've talked about all the advance notice I heard and read about Steinbrenner before I took the Yankees job. Everyone wanted to know what I was going to do when George did . . . whatever George was going to do. Why, I wondered, should I worry about a hypothetical? Where would that get me? The only sane approach is to deal with problems as they arise. Should people living in Los Angeles or San Francisco spend their days worrying about the next big earthquake? What would be the point?

This goes back to Key #4, on sustaining serenity. Fretting about what your boss might do tomorrow or next month will destroy your focus on the present. And the present—today's task or deal or game—is where you should live. It may help to keep your distance from all the clamor in your organization.

One of my concerns with the Yankees has been to prevent distractions in the clubhouse. Some people have said that I've acted as a buffer between George and the players. That's not quite accurate. George is the principal owner; he has the right to come into the Yankee clubhouse anytime he wants. If I tried to keep him out, I'd be creating tension, not relieving it. When he's in town, he will often come into the clubhouse and talk to the players. Sure, he'll make some critical comments. He may agitate Zimmer and the other coaches and trainers. For the most part, it's all good-natured stuff. He becomes one of the guys, ribbing his colleagues.

I *have* tried to create a clubhouse atmosphere in which

bruised feelings and controversies never get out of hand. I've said to my players, "George is the owner, he can do whatever he wants. You don't have to like it, but you do have to understand that it's his right. Let George have his say, take it seriously, but don't overreact to it, and it's over." This approach strikes a balance between deference and distance.

My players have taken my advice, and George has not had a negative influence on our clubhouse. If anything, he motivates people by challenging them. With the volatile Yankee teams of the seventies and eighties, players and managers would overreact to every slight, which led to a media feeding frenzy. Beat writers and broadcasters never had to worry whether they would have something to report the next day. The stories would go on and on, because people never knew how to keep it under control.

In my tenure, there was one minor exception, a clubhouse incident that got some play in the media. In early September of 1997, we were in second place in the division, and we weren't playing well. It was David Wells's first season as a Yankee, and he had lost several games in a row. George came into the clubhouse during one of Wells's rocky starts. He made some comments to Boomer that he didn't appreciate. Wells responded by complaining about lax security in right field. A fan had just reached over and caught a ball below the edge of the wall, and the ump mistakenly called it a home run. George and David exchanged some heated words.

Several players came to the dugout and told me what was happening. We had a laugh and thought that was the end of it. But someone leaked the incident to the media, and they ran the story as a clash of the titans. The press reported that

Boomer had threatened to punch Steinbrenner, and that George replied with a version of "make my day."

I wasn't there, so I don't know exactly what happened. But two weeks later, George released a tongue-in-cheek statement in response to the rumors. "I may be a grandfather of ten, but I work out three times a week with the trainers here in Tampa and they tell me that I'm in pretty good shape for an old relic," read the statement. He added a joke about rejecting offers for a heavyweight boxing match. "I've already turned down fighting on the undercard for the [Ted] Turner-[Rupert] Murdoch heavyweight fight."

I wish the story hadn't leaked, but we saw the humor in it, and so did George. The media uproar lasted only a day or two, and I'm sure it's because we knew how to let the story die on its own. If you don't blow things out of proportion, they won't explode in your face.

I've had enough experience with tough bosses to know that every challenge is relative. For instance, Ted Turner came into our clubhouse much more often than George. He wanted to be loved by the players, who got much more of his attention than his coaches and staff. Often, Ted would jump over the wall of the stands after the last out, then run through the dugout into the clubhouse. He was far more intrusive than Steinbrenner.

No matter what kind of boss you have, it's important to work the chain of command. Make wise use of staff members, middle managers, administrators—anyone in the organization who helps you optimize your efficiency. You can defuse difficulties with a tough boss by relying on these individuals.

With the Yankees, I've been fortunate to work with two

talented general managers, Bob Watson and Brian Cashman. Bob did a great job, but he had a harder time with George than Brian, in part because he was new to the organization. He hadn't been familiar with the Boss's way of doing things. When Brian was named GM in 1997, he'd been with the Yankees for ten years. He already had a good relationship with George and was well prepared to take the reins. I have relied on both Bob and Brian whenever I have issues regarding personnel or coaches that are, strictly speaking, not my business. I'd share my concerns or ideas, and Bob or Brian would take them into account when they talked with George. It's a proper and effective way to use the chain of command.

Cashman reminds me of my friend and former GM with the Cardinals, Dal Maxvill. Like Maxie, Cash is loyal, tough, and he's not a yes-man. He's extremely bright, and he has a rough edge that enables him to withstand the heat that comes with his territory. I turn to Cash with issues that need to be run by George, and he always uses good judgment about whether he or I should do the talking. Sometimes he'll say, "You may have a better chance with George on this one."

Maintaining your distance doesn't necessarily mean keeping your boss at arm's length. It's all about judgment, discretion, staying calm, and relying on others in your organization to keep things running smoothly. Watson and Cashman, for example, deserve a lot of credit for the fact that my working relationship with George has been so steady.

Distance is also a way to prevent your boss from getting under your skin. I'll never forget a phone call from George in mid-August 1996, when our huge twelve-game divisional lead had shrunk to eight games. It was the first time I ever heard panic in his voice. "Joe, if you blow this thing, I'll never let you forget it," he said. "You'll have to live with this for the rest of your life. You'll be another Ralph Branca." George was referring to 1951, when the Dodgers blew a thirteen-game lead to the Giants in mid-August. In the season's final game, Bobby Thomson put the dagger in their hearts with his world-famous homer against the Dodgers' pitcher, Branca.

These were strong words from the Boss, and I made a point of not dwelling on them. Distance and serenity. I was not about to let myself get undone by the comparison. My serenity was tested, however, when our lead shrank down to two-and-a-half games in early September. But we held on to win the division on September 25, when we beat the Milwaukee Brewers in the first game of a doubleheader. During the clubhouse celebration George called to congratulate me. I picked up the phone and said, "Hello, this is Bobby Thomson."

Let these illustrations be a guide for using distance to sustain a workable relationship with your employer. Don't overreact to your boss's behavior. Let unimportant controversies die a natural death. Use the chain of command. Don't let negative comments get under your skin. When combined with deference and dialogue, distance can help you maximize your efficiency—while staying on the best possible terms with your boss.

Maintain Open Dialogue

Many of the principles of Key #3, straight communication, apply to your dealings with bosses as well as employees.

But tough bosses often challenge you to develop your communications skills. How do you talk to a tough boss? It's a good question.

You have to gauge your boss's personality and needs. Your assessment will help you determine what kind of approach will work. Some bosses need to know everything you're doing. Others couldn't care less about operational details. Some are completely secure. Others need reassurance. Some need to be confronted. Others need to be soothed. Some have no sense of humor. Others respond to humor like nothing else.

Observe your boss so you can learn more about how he responds. Then put your knowledge to work. Not to manipulate, but to speak a language he can understand.

George Steinbrenner expects reassurance. He gets very uneasy as the stakes get higher in a pennant race or playoff series. Once I realized this, I took it upon myself to ease his worst fears.

The Yankees were soundly beaten by the Braves in Game One of the '96 World Series. After getting shellacked 12–1, there was talk about us being out of our league. And we were about to face Greg Maddux, arguably the best pitcher in the majors that year. George came into my office before Game Two and said, "This game is a must."

"Listen, we're liable to lose tonight," I said, keeping any hint of alarm out of my voice. "But then we're heading to Atlanta. That's my town. We'll win three games there, then come home and clinch it for you on Saturday." George looked at me as though I'd just landed from Mars.

History will record that my prediction was on the money.

It was nothing but an educated guess, of course, but I used it to calm down George. (Plus, I hadn't slept a whole lot, and I was just goofy enough to make such a statement.) I did want to prepare him for our likely loss in Game Two against Maddux. We were out of practice, having clinched early against Baltimore and sat out six days before the start of the Series. But I figured that we'd shake off the rust by Game Three in Altanta, when our starter would be David Cone, a big-game guy who could hand us our first win.

Here's my philosophy on reassurance: If you predict World War III, you'll upset the hell out of people. Plus, if you turn out to be wrong, they'll come after you. If you predict *no* World War III, you calm people down. And who's going to come after you? People dealing with life and death won't give a damn what you predicted.

I saw the value of this approach while in basic training in 1962, in the Air Force National Guard at Lackland Air Force Base in Texas. I was put in charge of fifty men. We were on a march one evening when some of the troops worried aloud about being sent into combat. The Cuban Missile Crisis had been unfolding at the time. I said, "Don't worry, we're not going to war." What did I have to lose by reassuring them?

After we lost Game Two by a score of 4–0, George's pessimism really took over. He told a mutual acquaintance, "We can't be embarrassed. If we lose, everything we've accomplished up until now won't mean a thing."

Before Game Three, I made sure to calm him once more. "Don't worry about it, we're going to be fine," I said. "I hope so," he replied. "I trust you."

We were more than fine, as it turned out. My players

made me look good by fulfilling my prediction. My ability to reassure George might have faded fast if we hadn't picked ourselves up off the mat and beaten the Braves to win the World Series. Fortunately, I had been able to use information and intuition to build some credibility with George. More important than being right about my prediction, however, was my intent to be positive, not only for George's sake, but for my players as well.

Luckily, the pattern that began in 1996 has continued. The 1998 Yankees confronted only one serious crisis, when we went down two games to one in the American League Championship Series against Cleveland. George was concerned, so he called me up to his suite in Cleveland.

"What do you think?" he said. "It all comes down to tonight," I replied. I had just seen my starter for the game, Orlando Hernandez, laughing and serving food to his friends in the coffee shop. I told George that we might get beaten, but it wouldn't be because El Duque couldn't handle the pressure. "I'll tell you one thing," I said. "If we do win tonight, we may not lose another game."

I hedged a little, because I knew that everything depended on El Duque's outing that night. But I did believe that a victory would give us the edge in the series. Steinbrenner was concerned, but he wasn't angry or antsy. He had a "whatever happens, happens" attitude, which was fairly out of character for the Boss. Fortunately, El Duque mowed down the Indians, and we won three straight games to take the series.

There was a somewhat different feel to my exchanges with George in 1998. I didn't have to reassure him quite as much. George was understandably concerned that all our accomplishments during the regular season would be disregarded if we didn't win the title. But he wasn't as excitable as he'd been in the past. He seemed more willing to put his faith in the hands of his manager, coaches, and players.

Carefully consider how you communicate with your boss. Have you really thought about what kind of dialogue best serves the relationship? If not, start today. Bring as much intelligence to this relationship as you bring to your daily work. Ultimately, the work itself will benefit. If I were clueless about how to manage my relationship with the principal owner, I would have a much harder time managing the team. I might not be able to manage at all.

A light touch is important. You have to have a decent sense of humor when you work for a tough boss. Use it to relieve the pressure. During one of my phone chats during the '96 season, I said, "George, how about after you fire me, you put Zim and me in the broadcast booth?" He howled with laughter.

Use dialogue to clarify confusion. What I say about team players is applicable to bosses: I don't expect them to agree with me, but I do want them to understand my decisions. Confusion leads to misunderstanding, and misunderstanding leads to conflict. You can prevent a load of trouble by making sure your meanings and actions are clearly understood.

Steinbrenner and I had one of those misunderstandings early in the 1997 season. We had fallen far behind the Baltimore Orioles in the divisional standings. I commented to reporters that our team should not concentrate so much on catching Baltimore. We should focus on winning games and getting to the postseason as a wild card—our overriding goal. Then I said, "I better be careful what I say, or the Boss will get on me." He did, telling the media that he feared I had given up on winning the division.

Soon afterward George showed up in my office. I brought up the subject. "I didn't mean that we can't catch Baltimore," I said. "But I don't want us worrying about them right now. We've got to keep our minds on reachable goals. We should play against ourselves and win as many games as possible. Then nobody can keep us out of the postseason."

George backtracked a bit, denying that he had taken exception to my remarks. In any event—most importantly—I had clarified what I meant. I think he got the message, because days later the media quoted him making the same points I had made in our meeting.

Deference and distance go a long way, but there's no doubt that success will do wonders for your dialogue with your boss. (A good relationship is vital, but no matter who your boss is, you still must produce.) Once you notch a few victories, the trust factor is instantly strengthened. Build your relationship with your boss over time, and as you achieve your shared goals the dialogue will become easier. Winning the World Series in 1996 made me that much more credible and trustworthy to my boss. He became more patient, more willing to accept my decisions at face value. Our relationship was further strengthened when he realized that I wasn't satisfied with winning only one World Series.

Winning has also brought out George's sensitive side. He cares so much about his team's fortunes, and he's been through so much turmoil over the years, that our successes in '96 and '98 overwhelmed him. When we wrote our ticket to the World Series by beating Baltimore in the '96 ALCS, he called me in the clubhouse and wept on the phone. An especially moving moment occurred in 1998 when George received the World Series trophy. Baseball commissioner Bud Selig, a dear old friend of George's, handed it to him as I stood by his side. He cried openly, and I got choked up, too. I suppose that George had a lot on his mind—the joy of such a perfect season, his friendship with Selig, his thoughts about possibly selling the team.

Bring these qualities to the dialogue with your tough boss: Awareness. Patience. Assertiveness. Humor. Honesty. Intelligence. Clarity. Courage. And don't forget those standbys, trust and respect. Take as much care with this important relationship as you would with a marriage or long-term friendship. Let it grow, change, and develop as a marriage or friendship would.

Deference, distance, and dialogue is like a recipe: It works when you use the right amounts of each. Too little deference, distance, or dialogue creates obvious problems; so does too much. Tough bosses present tough challenges, but you can meet them by relying on your common sense, day in and day out.

Torre's Winning Ways
Key #9: Dealing with Difficult Bosses III: Deference, Distance, and Dialogue

- **Display Deference**
  - Deference means loyalty and respect, not submissiveness.

- Don't broadcast your ongoing problems.
- Recognize that every boss, just like every employee, wants to be understood and treated with dignity.

- **Use Distance as a Strategy**
  - Don't overreact to your boss's behavior.
  - Let petty disputes and controversies die a natural death.
  - Use the chain of command to keep your relationship smooth.
  - Don't let harsh criticism or fear tactics get under your skin.

- **Maintain Open Dialogue**
  - Gauge your boss's personality and needs. Use this information as a guide to your communication.
  - If your boss is nervous or high-strung, perfect the art of reassurance.
  - Rely on humor and a light touch, if your boss is responsive.
  - Bring as much intelligence to your relationship with your boss as you bring to your work. Ultimately, the work itself will benefit.

CHAPTER 10 **Key #10: Steadiness and Small Bites: How to Handle Setbacks**

What's the best way to handle setbacks? Two of my keys are vital—serenity and optimism. Remaining calm, levelheaded, and positive helps you to bounce back from loss. When you're tense, or stuck in negative thinking, it becomes harder to focus on the job at hand. A vicious cycle is set in motion. A setback gets you down, your work suffers, you get more down, then you hit the wall. Serenity and optimism can break that cycle. They enable you to spring back from defeats with confidence.

But there's more you can do to handle setbacks. Develop the mindset of steadiness. Do so by recognizing that there *are* no triumphs without setbacks. The greatest champion can't be victorious every day. The most talented businessman or entrepreneur can't close every deal. You appreciate winning because you know the disappointment of loss—the defeats in your professional and personal life. Once you understand this, you are less likely to be brought down by one failure, or even a series of failures.

Baseball illustrates this perfectly. During the long 162-game baseball season, my players have to remain steady. (So do I.) I don't want a loss to get them too down, because there's a game the next day. And I don't want a victory to get them too high. Same reason. In baseball, slumps can stretch on for days or weeks. Go into a funk and you may only prolong the slump. Winning streaks can stretch on, too. But they last longer when you don't get so pleased with yourself that you become overconfident. Steadiness is a winner's mentality.

The need for steadiness is another reason why baseball is more like business and life than any other sport. Pro football, for example, requires intense week-long preparation for that one burst of high energy on Sunday afternoon. A hundred-and-sixty-two games over six months have the pace and rhythm of our work lives. Each day we confront a series of small challenges that eventually add up to something larger. But that something larger does not materialize for quite a while, until the end of a season or year, sometimes longer. We set long-range goals for ourselves—the deals, profits, promotions, campaigns, acquisitions—that come to fruition only when we string together a lot of successful days over many months. Just like baseball.

Steadiness is the quality of people who have their goals firmly in mind as they go about their business, knowing that bad days are par for the course, and good days are bricks in the foundation of that something larger.

I have developed a strategic approach to baseball that breeds steadiness. I call it the "small bites" approach, and you can apply it to any endeavor in business or life. Basically, the "small bites" philosophy is that winning results from an assembly of small elements over time. When you focus your attention on these elements, you can overcome the biggest obstacles, reach heights you thought were not possible. "Small bites" helps you rebound from setbacks, because you don't get overwhelmed by how daunting the task seems. Your goal is firmly in mind, but you focus on the little things you must do to win *today*.

Soon after we met, my wife, Ali, and I went on a vacation to the Grand Canyon. We started hiking from the base of the canyon, and I thought, "This isn't so bad." Then I looked up and realized it was straight up the rest of the way. I suddenly got so fatigued I didn't know if I could make it. I figured I better not look up, so I kept my gaze focused in front of me, step by step. I made it to the top, tired but no worse for the wear. That's small bites in a nutshell.

Small bites isn't a radical new idea. It's really an old idea, but I've made it practical—easier for you to apply when confronted with any serious challenge in your work life. In this chapter, I summarize this approach in two sections:

- Small Bites: The Winning Equation
- Right the Ship: Steadiness During Setbacks

Develop steadiness and use the small bites approach to bounce back from any setback, no matter the magnitude. Setbacks can affect your goals this week, this season, this year, or over the course of your career. Steadiness and small bites can help you handle them all.

Small Bites: The Winning Equation

Think of winning as a puzzle. When you put together a puzzle, the picture on the front of the box reminds you of your goal. But your job is to examine each piece and assemble the puzzle, piece by piece. Gradually, the picture emerges. Winning in baseball and business is no different. To achieve your "big" goal, you must assemble a large number of little accomplishments and make them fit perfectly together.

When you break down your goal into doable components, you can rise to any challenge.

The best example in my career is our 1996 World Series comeback. We lost the first two games against the Atlanta Braves by a combined score of 16–1. The Atlanta staff of John Smoltz, Greg Maddux, Tom Glavine, and Denny Neagle was considered a murderer's row of starting pitchers, and we'd already lost to Smoltz and Maddux in our ballpark. Our hitters had been stifled, while the Braves' hitters had been relentless. Andruw Jones, a rookie who'd played only 31 games in the majors, ripped two homers in Game One. We would play our next three games in Atlanta's Fulton County Stadium against their formidable starters on full rest. The media counted us out. George Steinbrenner was most concerned that we avoid the embarrassment of a sweep.

Sound overwhelming? It was, and there's no doubt I was concerned. But I remained optimistic. I wasn't close to giving up, and the reason involves the small bites approach. In my mind, I broke down our assignment into a series of challenges we could meet. I encouraged the team not to focus on the magnitude of the task ahead. Had they said to themselves, "Oh, God, we have to face Glavine, Neagle, Smoltz, and Maddux," they'd have been overwhelmed. Instead, they focused on one thing alone: winning Game Three.

I had to think small. If I worried about beating the Braves' starters, I, too, might have been overwhelmed. My goal was a bit more modest—get the starters out of the game so we could face their middle relievers. I liked our chances against the Braves' bullpen. One hurdle at a time.

One of my decisions on the eve of the World Series also gave me reason for hope. I had chosen David Cone to pitch Game Three, which I believe is pivotal in a best-of-seven series. Game Three is crucial whether you are up two games (a win makes you almost unbeatable), tied at one (a win gives you a critical edge), or down two games (a win keeps you in the series). Cone was familiar with Atlanta's stadium, having pitched there when he was with the Mets. More important, David had proven himself in high-pressure games. I knew he was going to have a big heart out there.

Cone did not disappoint. He pitched a gutsy game, allowing only one run and four hits in six innings. I've described how he pitched out of a bases-loaded jam in the sixth, showing once again his big-game ability. We beat the Braves 5–2, and we now trailed them two games to one.

By winning Game Three, we got the momentum to shift. Now we were the aggressors in the series.

The next step would be much harder. Like the series itself, Game Four, a postseason classic, was a monumental uphill battle. The game offers a microcosm of the small bites approach in action.

Kenny Rogers was our Game Four starter, and the way he

had been pitching, I suspected this might be a high-scoring game. We fell behind 4–0 in the second inning, and I decided to pull Rogers in the bottom of the third after he gave up two consecutive singles. I replaced him with Brian Boehringer, who allowed one run on a sacrifice fly but pitched well, setting down six straight batters. Reliever David Weathers gave up another run in the fifth, making the score 6–0.

We were only four innings from going down three games to one, a virtually impossible mountain to climb. But I wanted that out of my players' minds. When they came into the dugout after the fifth, I said for all to hear, "Let's cut their lead in half right here. One run at a time. Small bites. Let's put pressure on them."

As if on cue, Derek Jeter hit a bloop single that fell in front of the right fielder, Jermaine Dye. This came right after Jeter had hit a catchable fly toward the right-field line, but Dye's path was blocked by the umpire, so the ball dropped into foul territory. I saw this as a good sign, since we'd been getting more than our share of lucky breaks all season long. So many, in fact, that I was starting to wonder if we were a team of destiny. (In our Championship Series with Baltimore, we had won the first game with an assist from a twelve-year-old kid who reached over the right-field wall to grab a fly ball off Jeter's bat, pulling it into the stands. The umpire working right field, Richie Garcia, called it a home run. The infamous homer tied the game in the eighth, and we went on to win in the eleventh.)

With Jeter on base, Bernie Williams walked. Cecil Fielder ripped an opposite-field double to right-center, scoring both runners. I wanted the next batter, Charlie Hayes, to get a good hack, preferably hitting the ball toward right field so that Cecil could advance to third. Hayes did his job and then some—slapping the ball to right for a single that drove Fielder home.

We had cut the lead in half, just as I had hoped. We were doing the small things, and it was paying off. The term "little ball" is often used for the brand of baseball that depends on the bunt, hit-and-run, the stolen base, the sacrifice—anything to advance the runner. I'm a proponent of little ball, the small bites philosophy in practice. Your strategy is to think one run at a time, rather than trying to make up for a big deficit all at once with a flurry of home runs.

With the score 6–3, our right-handed reliever Jeff Nelson took care of his piece of the puzzle. Nellie kept us in the game with two innings of no-hit ball.

The eighth proved to be a major turning point in the series. We would face Mark Wohlers, the Brave's hard-throwing closer. Charlie Hayes led off the inning with a swinging bunt down the third-base line that started to go foul before making a right-hand turn into fair territory. Darryl Strawberry then singled, and Mariano Duncan hit a stinging ground ball to short, a surefire double-play ball. But Rafael Belliard misplayed the ball, getting only one out at second. Two men on, the tying run at the plate.

Our catcher Jimmy Leyritz was the batter, in a situation packed with pressure. He would face Wohlers, who throws as hard as any closer in the game. Leyritz promptly fouled off several of his heaters. Wohlers seemed to feel that Jimmy was on his fastball, so he decided to try using his slider, which is probably his third best pitch. With the count two and two, Wohlers threw his mistake pitch, a slider hung out over the plate. Leyritz drilled the pitch over the left-field fence for a three-run homer that tied the game at 6–6. It was such a dramatic home run that for a moment I went numb.

The score remained tied until the top of the tenth. The eighth and ninth innings were filled with managerial chess moves. I used Mike Aldrete as a pinch hitter in the eighth, and Andy Fox as a pinch runner for Cecil Fielder in the ninth. With the bases loaded and two outs in the ninth, I decided to stay with Mariano Duncan, even though he had been struggling with the bat. One reason was that we were playing in a National League park, where you can run yourself out of players by pinch hitting too often. With the score tied in the late innings, it was important that I save my best pinch-hitter—in this case, Wade Boggs—for a crucial spot. Duncan hit the ball hard, but it was caught by Jermaine Dye in right field. The chess match continued.

With two outs and nobody on base in the tenth, Braves' left-hander Steve Avery walked Tim Raines on four pitches. Derek Jeter slapped a single to left. We had the switch-hitting Bernie Williams up next, who is better as a right-handed hitter. Braves' manager Bobby Cox could turn Bernie around by bringing in a right-hander, or he could intentionally walk him to load the bases. Cox chose to walk Bernie.

This was the moment to pinch-hit Boggs, the future Hall-of-Famer. Boggsy is a patient, professional hitter with a great eye at the plate. Wade usually works the count, and he did just that. At two balls and two strikes, he refused to bite at a slider just barely off the plate. Ball three. With the count full, the bases loaded, and the game very possibly on the line,

Avery threw a fastball that wasn't close enough to tempt Wade. He held off, and the base-on-balls brought home the go-ahead run. As far as I was concerned, it was the greatest RBI of Wade's great career.

Charlie Hayes hit a soft pop-up toward first base, but Ryan Klesko seemed to lose the ball in the lights, and dropped it for an error. We had another run, and the score was now 8–6. One more small bite left—the bottom of the tenth. It was up to our relievers, Graeme Lloyd and John Wetteland. Lloyd, the big left-hander who never failed us in the post-season, promptly struck out the leadoff hitter, Klesko. Then I brought in Wetteland. John gave up a single to Andruw Jones, which made me jittery in the dugout—something that rarely happens. But John got a fly-ball out before giving us one final scare—a long fly ball that almost eluded the grasp of Tim Raines in left field. Tim fell backward and stumbled on the warning track as he caught the last out.

We celebrated in the clubhouse, hugging one another, amazed at what we had accomplished. It was the greatest comeback in a single game in Yankee postseason history. I could barely sleep that night. But I also never lost sight of our goal—winning the World Series.

The series was tied at two games apiece. While the momentum had definitely swung our way, the puzzle was still not complete. I have already described our taut 1–0 victory behind Andy Pettitte in Game Five. We went back to Yankee Stadium for Game Six, where we beat the Braves by a score of 3–2. It was one final, stirring victory in an unforgettable World Series. We had come back from being down two games to none to win three straight on their turf, then returned home to write the storybook ending.

People said that what we accomplished was improbable, and I guess it was. Analyze the comeback piece-by-piece, however, and it doesn't seem so unlikely. The small bites philosophy puts the unreachable within reach. Of course, it took sound strategy, great execution, and patience—with a sprinkling of luck for good measure. Putting aside the lucky breaks, these were factors we controlled by taking the right approach.

Players who are involved in a postseason series—whatever the sport—get constant questions about winning the championship. When they start thinking championship, they get distracted from the business at hand—today's game. I tell players to put blinders on, whether they're up or down in a series. If they're down, the blinders keep them from getting overwhelmed. If they're up, the blinders keep them from losing their focus. Too often, teams with the lead in a series suffer a big letdown the moment they lose a game. Maybe they've been too busy celebrating the championship that hasn't yet happened. Players should be so wrapped up in playoff games that they won't realize that they won the championship until someone taps them on the shoulder with the news: "Hey, it's over. You won it."

This rule applies to business. Don't think ahead to closing the deal. Tend to your knitting on the little things before you even think about tasting victory. When you do, someone will eventually tap you on the shoulder, surprising you with the good news.

Small bites is a kind of mathematical strategy, like figuring out the common denominator. You boil down your task to an acceptable number of problems, each one of which you can solve. In baseball, you chip away at large deficits by taking one inning at a time. You find an edge *this* inning against *this* pitcher with *these* batters and *these* guys available on your bench. Shoot for one run at a time, and the next thing you know, you're back in the game—or you've already won it.

It's an approach any businessman or woman can take. Break down your problem into bits and it won't overwhelm you. Setbacks won't feel insurmountable. Big dreams will seem within reach. Small bites can help executives, entrepreneurs, and managers to be visionaries, because their bold ideas no longer seem impossible.

Right the Ship: Steadiness During Setbacks

There are times in our work lives—and personal lives, too—when we don't want to get up in the morning. The obstacles seem too tough, the challenges too daunting. Perhaps we've suffered a serious setback, and the pain is still intense. As a result, we don't feel even close to 100 percent on the job. The instincts we've relied upon to succeed are no longer sharp. What do we do then?

The simple answer is, be patient. The pain of a setback at work and the pain of a personal loss are not that different. We need time to recover. When it comes to a professional failure, we must be patient with ourselves. We *will* get over it. We can even turn the setback into a plus by learning something from the experience. In the meantime, we still have to get out of bed. Whether in business or baseball, showing up should be automatic, something we don't even think about.

Steadiness is a form of maturity. Over time, we realize that we can accept our mistakes and grow, without losing confidence. Setbacks will make us feel bad, but we don't have to let them ruin our self-esteem. Not if we're patient. Not if we stop being too hard on ourselves.

One of my players who is hard on himself is Tino Martinez. Tino gets down during slumps, but he really beats himself up during the postseason. Despite his problems, Tino has shown how it's possible to overcome a significant setback.

Going into the 1998 World Series, Tino had only 1 RBI in 76 career playoff at-bats. When mired in a postseason slump, he seems to forget what a productive hitter he is. During his first three years with the Yankees, Tino has led the team in RBIs, and he's been our home-run leader two of those years.

While I repeatedly tell Tino, "Look at all those runs you've knocked in," I'm not always sure my comments sink in. During the first two rounds of the 1998 playoffs, Tino and I talked several times about his hitting woes. "I've always had this problem in the postseason," he said. "Tino, I don't accept that," I replied. "Sure, there's more pressure. But it's still just a ballgame." Tino's slumps are a mind-body problem. His hitting ability doesn't disappear; he gets into trouble only when he starts fighting himself.

We entered the '98 World Series having swept the Rangers in the divisional series and survived the Indians' tough challenge in the ALCS. While we were favored over the San Diego Padres, critics noted that our postseason hitting was far below our standards. Our team batting average against the Indians had been .218. Several guys, including Bernie Williams and Chuck Knoblauch, were stuck in slumps. But Tino was really struggling. His combined batting average during the 1998 division series and ALCS was .167, and the fans and the media were getting on Tino for another rough October.

The pressure in Game One was intense. The media put us on notice that our status as one of the great teams in baseball history was on the line. We were warned that the Padres' starter, Kevin Brown, would be our hitters' worst nightmare. If we lost the first game, we would surrender our home field advantage—and perhaps our psychological edge. While I didn't want us getting caught up in the media hype, we couldn't help but feel the pressure.

We were on the ropes early in Game One, and the pressur built with the Padres leading 5–2 going into the seventh. But the seventh changed everything. Brown got the first out, but Jorge Posada ripped a single to right. Ricky Ledee, who had doubled in the second to drive in our two runs, worked out a walk. Brown, who early in the game had been hit in the leg by a hard line drive off the bat of Chili Davis, was losing his command, and reliever Donne Wall replaced him.

Wall promptly fell behind Chuck Knoblauch with a 2–0 count. Chuck had been having his own postseason difficulties. His blunder in Game Two of the ALCS, in which he argued an umpire's call as the go-ahead run scored, made him the object of media ridicule. Chuck admitted his mistake at a press conference the next day, effectively putting the incident behind him. But he continued to struggle at the plate.

Wall was shaky, and his 2–0 pitch was straight down the middle. Chuck made solid contact, hitting a high fly ball down the left-field line. Greg Vaughn backed up to the wall, then jumped high in an attempt to grab the ball out of the stands. It drifted beyond his grasp. Chuck's three-run homer tied the game, and the 56,000 fans in Yankee Stadium erupted. It was a moment I'm sure Chuck will never forget. Any lingering bad taste over his mistake in the ALCS was washed away, for good.

The game was tied, but we were just getting started. Derek Jeter singled, knocking Wall out of the game. Left-handed reliever Mark Langston took over, getting Paul O'Neill to fly out. Jeter advanced on a wild pitch, Bernie Williams was intentionally walked, and Chili Davis worked out a walk. With bases loaded and two outs, Tino Martinez went up to the plate. Several of our guys yelled out to him, "This is your time."

Tino worked the count to two balls and two strikes. Langston then threw a knee-high fastball close to the outside corner. It was called a ball, and everyone in our dugout sighed with relief. With the count full, Langston had to throw a strike. Martinez took full advantage, slamming Langston's fastball high and deep into the upper deck in right field. His grand slam homer, which put us ahead 9–5, caused a frenzy in the Stadium. The crowd chanted his name in unison, and called him out onto the dugout steps. I was elated for Tino. He had finally gotten the monkey off his back.

The seven runs in the seventh inning put us over the top, and we went on to sweep the series for our second championship in three years. This one inning taught us something about the art of the comeback. Despite their difficult postseasons, both Knoblauch and Martinez came through with extraordinary displays of clutch hitting. Some people called it the "inning of redemption" for both men, though I don't see how either one had to be redeemed. Chuck had admitted his error, and Tino had made every effort to revive his bat.

Tino still gets down on himself, but he has become steadier. His breakthrough in Game One helped him set aside the idea that his postseason slumps are inevitable, that he can't rebound from a long-lasting setback. He's a bit more patient with himself, and I think that will pay dividends in the future.

Managers must be able to put themselves in their employees' shoes. I admit one of my strengths as a manager— I was a player and I understand what players go through. I know what Tino feels when he's struggling. I appreciate Paul O'Neill's frustration. I can sympathize with Bernie Williams when he feels he let himself and the team down. My advice tends to carry a little extra weight with my players because they know I speak from experience.

I had my share of setbacks as a player, to be sure. I won the National League Most Valuable Player Award in 1971 with a .363 batting average and 137 RBIs. At the end of that same year I was very active in the players union, which initiated a strike that lasted into the first week of the regular season. But my union activity didn't sit well with the fans. On opening day of the 1972 season, I was introduced in St. Louis as the MVP, only to hear a loud chorus of boos. It was one of the more painful moments of my career.

The year started on a bad note and went downhill from there. I was straining to duplicate my MVP season, and at the same time my second marriage was falling apart. Tensions and negative thoughts began to affect my game. My 1972 numbers were respectable—a .289 batting average with 81 RBIs—but far below the standard I set for myself based on the previous year. I continued to be hard on myself, and though I still had some years ahead of me, my career as a player declined.

My experience allows me to talk to my players with a mixture of first-hand knowledge, understanding, and directness. I don't preach or condescend because I know how hard it can be. I understand what it means to get stuck in a rut, and I'll do whatever I can to help them get back on track. Some players need a pat on the back; others need a tactful shove.

As a manager, try to comprehend your employees' problems and concerns from the inside out. Even if you have not been in their same position, imagine how you might feel and behave in their place. You'll be much more successful as you try to help them overcome setbacks.

You can apply steadiness and small bites to big problems—including major career challenges or setbacks. Come up with an action plan to help you achieve long-range goals, and break down your plan into chunks you can handle. For instance, if you want to form your own Internet company, map out your strategy with a time line—here's where I want to be in three months, six months, two years, and so forth. If you miss a mark, rewrite your time line to make it more realistic. Use small bites as a flexible strategy, not a rigid one that makes you feel worse whenever you don't master a short-term goal.

People can use small bites to deal with long-range career

challenges, but it takes patience and maturity. (I know, because I waited longer than any other major league player or manager to get to the World Series.) This is hard for twenty-five-year-olds to do, because they want everything right now. (Derek Jeter is an exception to the rule.) We have to work in the bowels of the ship before we can rise to ship captain. Without patience, our dreams and plans are just a collection of nice fantasies. *With* patience, and a smart plan broken down into small bites, our dreams become attainable.

Torre's Winning Ways
Key #10: Steadiness and Small Bites: How to Handle Setbacks

- Recognize that there are no triumphs without setbacks. Understand this, and you're less likely to be brought down by one failure, or a series of disappointments.

- **Small Bites: The Winning Equation**
  - Think of winning as a puzzle. To achieve a "big" goal, assemble a large number of little accomplishments and make them fit perfectly together.
  - Boil down your task to an acceptable number of problems and solve them, one at a time.
  - Don't focus on closing a deal or winning an award—concentrate so completely on the small bites that you'll need someone to tell you that you've achieved a victory.

- **Right the Ship: Steadiness During Setbacks**
  - When you've suffered a serious setback, be patient—you will be able to recover.
  - Put yourself in your employees' shoes as you help them overcome setbacks. Don't preach or condescend; find out what kind of support they need.
  - Approach long-range career setbacks with patience, maturity, and a smart plan broken down into achievable goals.

CHAPTER 11 **Key #11: Caring,
Conviction, and
Commitment: The
Three C's to Success**

You can get by in sports and business with
good performance. Go to work, do your job efficiently, col-
lect your paycheck, live your life. But there's an extra
dimension that separates winners from just plain good per-
formers. Through my years in baseball, I've found that it
comes down to three basic qualities: caring, conviction, and
commitment.

Winners care deeply about the quality of their work.
They care about their teammates. They go about their jobs
with the utmost conviction. And they are totally committed
to the goals they've set for themselves. Anyone who demon-
strates these three C's is a success, as far as I'm concerned.
Even if they never earn medals, rings, awards, or multimillion-dollar contracts.

The championships and mega-deals of our dreams are
by-products of individual hard work and solid, unselfish
teamwork. This requires immense drive and energy. The
fuel? Caring, conviction, and commitment.

The 1998 Yankees had caring, conviction, and commitment to burn. They were (and are) a group of dedicated professionals who cared about getting to the World Series, and they cared about each other. They were so committed to winning that they checked their egos at the clubhouse door. In today's big-money world of sports, players typically put their own interests above everything else. Playing time is everything. Commercial endorsements are a close second. My players didn't gripe about playing time. They all wanted to contribute, but each one respected my judgments regarding day-to-day decisions. A manager could not ask for a better group of team players.

How did we win 125 games in one season? Why have we been discussed as one of the greatest baseball teams of all time? We were an immensely talented group. But I think it was the intangibles that set us apart. My players embodied all the keys needed for success as team players—self-knowledge; fairness, trust, and respect; communication; serenity; optimism; intuition; steadiness; sacrifice, and the three C's. I did my bit to preach these qualities, but these guys already had them in spades. Bring together a group like that, and you have the opportunity to accomplish things you never dreamed possible. 1998 was such a year.

In this Key, I offer guidelines to building the three C's in these sections:

- Caring: The Ties That Bind
- Conviction: The Will to Succeed
- Commitment: Building Your Foundation

Caring, conviction, and commitment are every bit as essential for corporate teams or families. The three C's keep teams together, regardless of their makeup or the goals they share. Trust, fairness, and respect are factors that strengthen communication and build teamwork. But caring, conviction, and commitment motivate us to work harder, to cooperate with one another, to keep driving until we reach our goals.

Caring: The Ties That Bind

Remember, two aspects of caring help us to succeed: caring about our goals and dreams, and caring for our teammates, without whom we'll never achieve anything. Both types are integral to success.

Caring creates camaraderie, which can only be good for teamwork. I'm not saying that teammates have to love or even like each other. The Oakland Athletics teams of the 1970s had many scuffles in their clubhouse, but that didn't stop them from winning three world championships. What *is* required among team players is professionalism and respect. The Yankee teams in all my four years have certainly shown both of these qualities.

But we also have real togetherness, which is a bonus. Our players really like one another. They enjoy one another's company in the clubhouse and the dugout. Their joking is always in a spirit of fun. Derek Jeter and Paul O'Neill have a great time with Don Zimmer, matching wits and trading insults. In June 1999, our versatile utility infielder, Luis Sojo, filled in for Jeter, who had suffered a leg cramp in the hot Baltimore sun. Before his last at-bat in the ninth, Luis half-jokingly guaranteed a shot out of the park. Jeter and the other guys within earshot had a good laugh, since Sojo hadn't hit a home run in two years. He knocked the ball into the left-field seats, then managed to keep a straight face as he rounded the bases. But as he approached the dugout, he had a huge smile on his face, and the guys who had doubted him were in stitches.

But a team's togetherness is not just fun and games. The Yankees have shown that. They genuinely love and care for one another. They demonstrated that throughout the 1998 season, when they scaled the heights of baseball success, and again in 1999. Has this helped us win? While I know that teams can win without strong bonds, I do think it has added a dimension for us. We've weathered some difficult storms because we know we can count on one another.

This is a realistic model for the business world: You can succeed as long as you and your teammates show professionalism and respect. It isn't necessary to love your colleagues, as long as you communicate well and develop a level of respect. But if you happen to click as a group, your teamwork and commitment may even be strengthened.

Several moments in 1998 capture the closeness among our players. Darryl Strawberry was diagnosed with colon cancer after the second game of our divisional series against the Rangers. We were down in Arlington while Darryl was back in New York preparing for surgery. Given his symptoms, we worried that he might have cancer, but the news was still devastating. There was a sense of loss and emptiness in the clubhouse. Darryl had emerged as a team leader, and a potent offensive force for our club. Above all, he established many friendships, and each one of us was concerned about his well-being. People said many prayers for Darryl during the days before his surgery, which took place the morning after our third game against Texas.

Before his operation, Darryl and his wife, Charisse, made a forty-five-second videotape with a message for us. NBC wanted to come into our clubhouse and tape the players watching the videotape. I thought this would turn the event into a carnival, so I adamantly refused to let them in. The team huddled around the clubhouse television and listened to Darryl deliver an emotional yet upbeat message. We were all moved. He was on the verge of tears, but when he signed off he got this glint in his eye. "Go get 'em tonight, guys. Get 'em." Everyone broke up laughing.

We took some inspiration from Darryl. Not that we needed any added motivation, but I think guys were fired up, wanting to win a championship for him. (Our equipment manager, Rob Cucuzza, had Darryl's number 39 sewn into the back of our caps.) Darryl's diagnosis also gave us pause to think about the game we were playing as compared to the one he was playing. We'd been feeling the pressure of living up to our record-breaking season, and suddenly we had an entirely different perspective on baseball and life. Darryl's situation was terribly disturbing, but in a strange way it relieved some of our postseason pressure. The games also gave us a chance to block out our fears and concerns for a few hours.

We beat Texas in three straight games. After a long rain delay, the final game on Friday went deep into the night. Afterward, the players sprayed champagne and beer in the clubhouse, both to celebrate our victory and to honor Darryl. The players let loose, and with all our pent-up emotions, I thought it was good therapy.

Our background with Darryl may help explain why we haven't dismissed him in the aftermath of his arrest in Tampa before the start of the 1999 season. Strawberry is a friend to many of us, and we are first and foremost concerned for his welfare. We hope that he stays healthy and is able to return to doing what he loves—playing baseball.

No matter what kind of job you hold, at times during your career a coworker will be stricken, or a family member will be sick or suffering. Our experience with Darryl may be instructive. First, talk with your teammates. Our players were very open with each other about their fear and sadness, and I think it helped them. Find ways to honor your colleague or family member. Rededicate yourself to goals that really matter. Develop a proper perspective on what's important. Let work become a refuge from grief or anxiety. Rely on prayer or any other psychological or spiritual approach that gives you comfort.

Throughout the current 1999 season, our players have had their share of worries about loved ones who are sick. Andy Pettitte's father continues to struggle with heart disease. Scott Brosius's dad is fighting prostate cancer. Paul O'Neill's father has undergone surgery for heart problems. Chuck Knoblauch's dad has a severe form of Alzheimer's disease. We were all concerned about Don Zimmer's terrible knee pain, which would only be relieved by replacement surgery. Add my own diagnosis of prostate cancer to the list, and it has not been an easy year on the personal front. Each of these players has his teammates' understanding and support, and each has done his best to handle his situations without letting it affect his on-field performance.

Another incident during the 1998 postseason said a lot about our club. In Game Two of the ALCS against the Indians, the game was tied at 1–1 in the twelfth when Chuck Knoblauch argued an umpire's call instead of focusing on the play. (I fully describe the play in chapter 4.) As a result, the Indians scored the go-ahead run. Chuck was booed by the fans and ridiculed by the media, and we had a major controversy on our hands.

The uproar could have distracted Chuck and the rest of us from the job we had to do. It was a critical moment in the ALCS, especially since we lost the next game and found ourselves in a do-or-die situation. Here is where our team togetherness really made a difference. The players supported him both privately and publicly, letting the media know that they were in Chuck's corner. If he'd made a mistake, it was forgivable. (I made similar comments to him when we spoke.) There were no critical words, no divisiveness, no backbiting. Not even a hint. I think this support really helped Chuck, who came to the wise decision to face the media and acknowledge his mistake, putting the incident behind him.

Our workmates are going to make mistakes. We, too, will experience embarrassing moments on the job. When colleagues band together to support someone who's screwed up, it's not just the individual who feels better. The team is strengthened. Teammates who offer support know full well that it could be them next time. Do employees who keep committing errors need to be confronted? Sure, depending on the type of errors. But what kind of confrontation helps? As I said in chapter 3, screaming and pointing fingers rarely does. Clear criticism can be useful, but that should come more often from a manager than from teammates. The most helpful thing teammates can offer is understanding.

We can also support our colleagues and workers by taking responsibility for mistakes that may have made their job harder. This happens all the time in baseball and in business. During the 1998 season, Andy Pettitte was enduring a rough stretch on the mound, giving up many runs in chunks in the early innings of games. In one game, Andy got in trouble in the third inning, with runners on second and third and nobody out. I brought the infield in, hoping to protect against even one run. Andy seemed to lose his composure, and before the inning was out, we were down 5–0. My strategy certainly hadn't worked.

Mel Stottlemyre and I sat down with Andy afterward to discuss his difficulties. Our main message to him was that you can't be perfect. He was trying to hit the corners too precisely, hoping to keep batters from hitting the ball. You do that and you fall behind in the count, which is the biggest problem for pitchers in a rut. When Andy would fall into this trap, he'd try to prevent a single run from scoring.

But I had to apologize to Andy for contributing to the problem when I brought the infield in during the game we'd just lost. "I take the blame for that," I said. "If I had played the infield back, I would in essence have told you to go ahead and give up the run. Just get an out and keep things from getting out of hand." Instead, I had sent Andy the wrong signal—

that he should prevent even one run from scoring. By taking responsibility for my mistake, I hoped to take some of the weight off his shoulders, and give him a clearer picture of what we expected from him. It's all about taking responsibility—and being supportive.

My players were very supportive of me when, during spring training of 1999, I first told them I had been diagnosed with prostate cancer, and explained my surgery. I felt their warmth and concern. As soon as I was strong enough, I began showing up at the ballpark for all our home games. I thought this would lessen their worries and keep up a sense of continuity. I figured it would be more distracting if I disappeared completely and then showed up one day to manage. By the time I did return, on May 18, 1999, in Boston, it was just a matter of putting on the uniform and getting back to work—closing the circle.

Conviction: The Will to Succeed

It was my first team meeting during spring training, during my first year as Yankee manager, 1996. I scanned the eyes of each player to see how my short speech was going over. Nobody was distracted. Everyone listened intently. I had the sense that this group was serious about winning.

I had laid it on the line with them. "Every one of my coaches have been to the World Series," I said. "But I haven't. I plan to rectify that this year. I'm determined as hell to get there."

I pledged to the team that I wouldn't manage through the media. If I had something significant to say, they would hear it from me first. "I'm going to try to eliminate tension on this team and in the clubhouse," I said. "The one thing that concerns me is how we perform on the field, and I'm going to make it as free of tension and distractions as possible so we can devote our energies to that."

None of us could have known that 1996 would be the year in which the dream came true. But I knew I was determined, and I knew this group of guys would take up my challenge. Many of them—Williams, Jeter, O'Neill, Cone, Rivera, Martinez, and Pettitte, among others—are still with the club, and they've led us to two championships in three years.

Conviction is the will to succeed. Again, it's an intangible, but one we can cultivate within ourselves. You may have a comfortable workplace with friendly colleagues, but if you don't have conviction—total determination to achieve your goal—you still won't be successful. It's up to you and your teammates to make it work.

To capture what I mean by conviction, I use the analogy of a burning house. Let's say there's an object in your home—an heirloom—that means a great deal to you. It's a hefty piece of furniture, one you were never able to move. Your house catches fire, and you instantly lift the piece and get it out of there. You become strong beyond your normal capabilities.

When you want something badly enough, you may suddenly discover abilities you never knew you had. Conviction—determination is another good word—enables us to accomplish things we always assumed were impossible.

As a manager, there have been times when I tried to inspire conviction in my players. One occurred during the middle of the 1997 season, which did not get off to a smooth start. We all felt the tension in the clubhouse. Before spring training, Cecil Fielder and Charlie Hayes had demanded to be traded. Cecil was frustrated by a contractual dispute. Charlie was not happy being platooned at third base with Wade Boggs. Boggs never complained, but many of us felt uncomfortable having a player of his stature warming the bench so much of the time. Pitcher Kenny Rogers, who always had problems with his confidence, continued to feel the pressure of playing in New York, where mistakes get magnified by the media.

We never had a breakdown of respect. But we did have guys with different agendas, so the clubhouse chemistry wasn't great. Early in the season, I called a team meeting. "There's something wrong here," I said. "So let's get it out in the open." I asked the players for their opinions and got some good feedback. The meeting got people thinking, and eventually the players put their personal agendas on the back burner and became more professional.

Afterward, there was less grumbling and more conviction. At the All-Star break, we were a respectable eleven games over .500, but we finished the season thirty games over—eight games better than in 1996. Despite our improved record in 1997, we fell short in the division to Baltimore while clinching the wild card slot in the playoffs.

Given the difficulties we faced in 1997, I am more proud of my managerial work that year than any other. We were able to set aside our conflicts and sustain a total effort. We lost our five-game divisional series to Cleveland, but by the thinnest of margins, coming up one run short in both Games Four and Five. Despite this ending, I have no regrets about

1997, and I give our team credit for the way they battled during their stretch run.

Something extraordinary came out of our disappointment. Our core group of players returned in 1998 with a renewed conviction to win another championship. They had been so stunned by the Cleveland series–the loss left them with such an empty feeling–that they vowed to themselves to come back and win it all. The atmosphere in spring training of 1998 was special–a combination of utter determination and looseness unlike any I had seen before. They were able to keep up this relaxed confidence throughout our record-setting season.

In chapter 4, I talked about taking control where you can and letting go of the rest. In business endeavors, you *can* control how much conviction you bring to your work. You can draw conviction from many sources, including from disappointment. If you get in the right frame of mind, nothing can rouse your determination like a stinging defeat. But it all starts with fire in the belly–the desire and will to succeed.

Commitment: Build Your Foundation

When you are committed to your work, it should be the most important thing you are doing at that moment. Many of us are driven by the desire for wealth, and that's fine. But it's awfully difficult to commit yourself to your job when the work itself does not inspire passion. I see this problem in some ballplayers (not on my team) whose actions speak these words, "Oh, I'm making five million dollars, so I must be successful."

Key #11: The Three C's to Success

Don't let your paycheck determine how you approach your work—or how you feel about yourself. If you make less than you want to, don't let that destroy your commitment. If you make a sizable salary, don't become complacent like the five million-dollar ballplayer. (You don't have to make millions to become complacent; it can happen to anyone who is financially comfortable.) Don't ever forget how hard you worked getting there. That's why it's important to separate the drive for excellence from the drive for wealth. You can have both motivations—just don't get them mixed up. Players must realize that they'll be judged on how they play, not how much they play *for*.

After we broke the American League record for wins in 1998, people asked me if the season would still be special if we didn't win the World Series. My answer was yes. It would not have been *as* special, because people would have discounted our accomplishments. But it was important for me and my players to recognize the value of what we had accomplished, championship or no championship.

You may ask: Are you saying that winning is not the most important thing? I do think it's most important. I'm proud that our 1998 team set the A.L. record for most wins, 114. But that doesn't mean our achievements are worthless unless we get that brass ring. Yes, winning is the ultimate goal. But getting the most out of your ability is all you can do. Despite what many motivational experts say, you can't always win! Even being super-talented and committed is no guarantee of victory. The breaks are not always going to go your way. When you're not winning, you can continue to be motivated to prove that you belong in the winner's circle.

When you have total commitment, you don't want to accept anything less than victory. That's healthy. But you can also value your accomplishments, both as an individual and as part of a team, even when you don't get rewarded. Baseball illustrates this point perfectly. There are thirty major league teams with twenty-five players each, the best baseball players in the world. Every year only twenty-five guys can call themselves world champions. Fifty make it to the World Series. Are the other seven hundred baseball players supposed to feel like losers?

Our emphasis on winning can be a double-edged sword. If we use it to stoke our passion and conviction, it's a plus. If we use it to beat ourselves up, it's a negative. We need to be passionate about winning, but in the right way. Little League dads who scream at their kids for making errors have the wrong take on winning. We should use the goal of victory as a carrot, not a stick.

Another reason to recognize your achievements: They give you something to build on. When your self-worth is totally based on winning, you may be less likely to *become* a winner. How so? As each year passes that you don't win, you lose sight of your strengths and your self-esteem. This leaves you with nothing to build on.

How many young players enter the major league as superstars? Very few. How many expansion teams win championships in their first year or two? None. We all need time to develop. Every year you should acknowledge your positive steps forward, while working hard to improve every aspect of your work. Know that you're building your foundation for future success. As the manager of three teams that never made it to the World Series, I was building my own foundation. I didn't always know it, since I was struggling to do the best job possible. I now know, looking back, how much I was learning and growing as a manager—without winning any rings. In his recent book, *The Perfect Season,* my old friend Tim McCarver pointed out that I joined the Yankees at the exact right time. "He was a bottle of wine, perfectly aged," Tim wrote. "It was time to pop the cork."

Building your foundation even when you aren't winning is a powerful form of commitment. You improve your chances of *becoming* a winner when you take this long view. Once you do start winning, your commitment is only strengthened. You have validation for *yourself* that your faith and hard work were all worthwhile. You stuck by your beliefs and principles and never counted yourself out. I can tell you from personal experience, this makes victory so much sweeter.

Torre's Winning Ways
Key #11: Caring, Conviction, and Commitment: The Three C's to Success

- **Caring: The Ties That Bind**
  - Two aspects of caring help us succeed: caring about our dreams and goals, and caring about our teammates.
  - Caring creates camaraderie, which may not be necessary for the team's success but which can improve teamwork.
  - You can succeed as long as you and your teammates show professionalism and respect.

- Offer support to teammates dealing with illness or family problems; seek support if you are dealing with these problems.

- **Conviction: The Will to Succeed**
  - Conviction, or the will to succeed, is an intangible quality we can cultivate within ourselves.
  - The combination of utter determination and a relaxed approach to your work is a pathway to success.
  - Draw conviction from any source necessary—including your disappointment over defeats. Let them spur you on.

- **Commitment: Build Your Foundation**
  - To build commitment, passion about your work should take precedence over other factors.
  - Don't let your paycheck—whether you consider it small or large—determine your approach to your work.
  - You build commitment when you value your accomplishments as an individual and team member—even if you don't get rewarded.

CHAPTER 12 **Key #12: The Game of Life: Sacrifice Is Not Just a Bunt**

I am often struck by how much I have learned about life from baseball. The qualities that lead to success in this graceful sport are no different from the ones that lead to success in business or family or any relationships. Steadiness, optimism, conviction, and commitment are at the top of the list. As I've said, I have applied the lessons of baseball to life, but I have also applied lessons of life to baseball.

Everyone brings their own life experiences to bear in their work, and many of the life lessons I've relied upon as a baseball player and manager come from my family life: Respect for authority. Trust as the basic currency of relationships. Open communication. Regard for people's dignity. The value of sacrifice.

In some cases we pick up good work habits and principles of leadership directly from parents or brothers and sisters. In other instances we go against their teachings. For instance, I learned to respect authority from my brothers, one of whom was a policeman and family man, the other a major league ballplayer. But I learned the value of serenity and fairness by turning away from the example of my father, who was prone to violent outbursts.

Family is a good model for business relationships and corporate affairs. What values do we bring to our job? How de we conduct our work relationships? How do we relate to authority? What kind of leadership skills do we possess? When we bring positive values and strengths we developed in our families to our work, we're bound to succeed. I show how this is possible in the following three sections:

- Sacrifice Is Not Just a Bunt
- Natural Born Leaders
- The Team as Family

This final key—the game of life—shows how you can apply the wisdom acquired in your family and from lifelong experience to your work life. Executives, managers, and team players can draw upon their own stockpile of life lessons as they strive for excellence. I'll start with two qualities I have applied from life to baseball—sacrifice and leadership. I'll finish by discussing how great teams are built upon the same principles as families.

Sacrifice Is Not Just a Bunt

Sacrifice in baseball refers to a play in which a batter lays down a bunt to advance a runner. Though he may reach base safely, the play is not designed for that. When he makes an out, he gives himself up for a cause—moving the runner into scoring position. Giving yourself up for the greater good—that's the essence of sacrifice. In baseball—and business—sacrifice is not just a bunt.

Ballplayers must often give themselves up in many ways to help the team succeed. Frequently, though, team players in baseball—or business—make the mistake of assuming that sacrifice means their personal goals will suffer. Not so. The 1998 Yankees, and many other storied franchises in team sports, have proven that players who sacrifice for the team get rewarded in the end. When you reach heights of achievement, the glory rubs off on everybody. People will long remember our '98 team, and diehard baseball fans came to appreciate the contributions of all twenty-five players. Even though baseball is a game based on individual achievements, an "anything I can do to help the team win" approach is the right frame of mind.

Sacrifice in business is no different. When you make sacrifices for the team—putting aside your needs for free time or personal glory—you advance your shared goals and give your company a better chance to succeed. People should get credit for their individual achievements, no question. But I've seen what happens when a team's watchword is sacrifice—everybody benefits.

On my team, a great example of someone who understands sacrifice is Joe Girardi. Joe is our backup catcher, and as I mentioned in chapter 8, I lobbied George Steinbrenner to hire him, mainly because of his defensive skills. But I also sensed that Joe, who had already played for two postseason contenders, was a winner. Girardi has since proven himself a natural leader, and one of the most unselfish players I've ever managed. If you just looked at his batting statistics you might pass him by, but what's most impressive are his intangible qualities—in the clubhouse, with our pitching staff.

We have a young player, Jorge Posada, who has gradually emerged as our number one catcher. Jorge is very talented and he has a live bat, though his offensive and defensive games are still inconsistent. Girardi has willingly taken a backseat to Jorge when it comes to playing time. But Joe has gone the extra mile by being his mentor. He teaches Jorge how to handle pitchers, working with him on the fundamentals of calling a game. As Posada improves, Joe may get even less playing time, but that doesn't stop him from making the sacrifice. He really cares for Jorge, and he'll do anything to help us win.

When you have team players like Girardi, there's no telling what you can accomplish. Someone like Joe doesn't ask for any thanks, but executives and managers should show their appreciation to employees who make such sacrifices. Most people want some recognition, and by giving it you motivate them to continue. This strengthens the fabric of your team. Likewise, employees who sacrifice should remind themselves that the team's triumphs—which they help bring about—can only advance their career.

When I managed the St. Louis Cardinals, there were times when I had trouble getting across my message about sacrifice. I tried everything. During one spring training, I even resorted to having players fill out forms listing their goals. Everyone wrote down "winning," but I doubted that half of them knew what winning was all about. I know they wanted to win, but they didn't understand the sacrifices involved.

Key #12: The Game of Life

We have guys on the Yankees who astound me with their willingness to sacrifice their minds and bodies for the cause of winning. Derek Jeter is one. He never considers a day off to be an option—that's the kind of kid he is. Just before the All-Star break in 1999, Derek was hit by a pitch several times, leaving him with a nasty contusion on his arm and a bruise on his side. There wasn't a chance he would miss a game, but when his leg cramped during hot weather, I decided to rest him. I can tell you that Derek would have preferred to play.

Whether your job requires physical or mental stamina, there are times when sacrifice and teamwork call upon you to put your mind and body on the line, so to speak. Think of the professionals who are willing, at various times in their careers, to work long hours, sacrificing sleep for the greater good. Doctors, paramedics, and lawyers do it all the time. Policemen and firemen often risk their lives. You have to take care of your physical health, but when you have a chance to accomplish something important—to help your team turn a vision into a reality—you ought to be willing to stretch yourself.

Sacrifice is also an attitude. I tell certain players who are struggling at the plate to forget about personal statistics, just think about winning. Don't attempt to compensate for a drought by trying to get four hits or hitting a home run. Concentrate on doing what it takes to win, whether it's a hit-and-run, a stolen base, moving a runner over, or a sacrifice. You take a lot of pressure off yourself that way.

Don't think of sacrifice as just a nice-guy approach to winning approval from your superiors. Whatever your profession, sacrifice is a hard-nosed, smart way to succeed by lifting up your teammates and yourself at the same time.

Natural Born Leaders

Most of us have some in-born leadership skills, though we don't always know it. I started to become aware of mine during my stint in 1962 in the Air Force National Guard at Lackland Air Force Base in Texas. They put me in charge of fifty men, perhaps because I was a major league ballplayer. Once I was put into that situation—with men looking to me for leadership—I began to think that maybe I had the goods.

My awareness grew after I joined the St. Louis Cardinals as a player in 1969. Until I was named team captain in 1970, I had not fully realized that my teammates and coaches saw me as a leader. The fact that I'd joined this successful organization, with so many classy professionals, and received this honor after having only been there one year, made me think seriously about myself as a leader. By the time I was named player/manager of the Mets in 1977, the transition to manager seemed natural.

The quality of leadership can be hard to define, since some of it relates to personality. The twelve keys capture most of the characteristics of effective leaders, and you can build each one into your own work life, no matter where you are on the corporate totem pole. But what about the intangibles? One of the best ways to pick up leadership qualities is to draw from the leaders in your midst. Ask yourself who in your work life—or among your family, friends, or teachers—strikes you as being a great leader. Observe how they go about their business, try to put your finger on what makes them inspiring leaders.

Many of my players are leaders. I am pleased by how

many men of character I have been fortunate to have on my team. Let me describe just a few, and perhaps you can draw from their examples.

Derek Jeter turned twenty-five during the 1999 season, but he already has the leadership qualities of someone a lot more experienced. At his young age, players already look up to him, and it's not because he's such a good player. It's because he handles being so good so remarkably well.

Derek impressed me right from the start in 1996, his rookie year. He already showed poise beyond his years. Before spring training I announced that Jeter would be my starting shortstop over Tony Fernandez. But when the press asked him about it, he said, "I'm going to get an *opportunity* to play shortstop." He wasn't taking anything for granted then, and he still doesn't.

I still remember a game that year in Chicago in which Jeter made a base-running mistake that contributed to a loss. With the power-hitting Cecil Fielder at the plate, Derek tried to steal third base in the eighth inning with two outs and us behind by a run. This was not a good gamble, because you shouldn't make the first or third out at third base. He was thrown out. I was mad, but also upset with myself for not giving him the stop sign. I couldn't expect a rookie to know that he should let Fielder hit. But in the heat of the moment, I thought I'd better not go over to him—I didn't want to rattle him. I told myself to calm down, he's just a kid. Next thing I know, Jeter sat himself down between Zimmer and me in the dugout so he could take his medicine. I just playfully hit him in the back of the head, and it was over.

Three years later, Derek is no longer a rising star, he's

more like a shooting star. Not only has he improved as a baseball player, he continues to handle the massive media attention with maturity. Every month the attention grows; he graces more magazine covers, gets more endorsement offers. He's virtually treated like a rock star. Yet none of this has affected Derek's attitude or his work habits. He's always the same—cool, dedicated, unflappable, focused. Despite everything, he keeps getting better and better as a shortstop and a hitter. He brings both a kid's joy and a mature man's judgment to his game. His 1999 season has all the makings of an MVP year.

How has Derek managed all this? I think it's his upbringing. He comes from a great family with two loving and supportive parents. That simple. When you observe Jeter as I have these past few years, one word comes right to mind—respect. He shows respect for everyone in his midst, and he earns respect from others.

While Jeter is a great example of leadership qualities in raw youth, David Cone, at thirty-six, represents qualities gained through experience. Cone has been a top pitcher in the majors for thirteen seasons. He has undergone multiple surgeries on his throwing arm, including a delicate operation in '96 to repair an aneurysm in the region of his armpit. He doesn't admit it, but every time he comes back to the pitcher's mound, he cannot know for sure if he'll ever pick up a ball again.

Anytime a player like David gets out there and puts his reputation, his career, and his health on the line, he automatically earns people's admiration. He has everyone's respect by virtue of his example, and I think that's true of most leaders. He's also very bright and articulate, which helps him a lot with the media. David is never afraid to stand up and talk to the press after a bad outing. Many players handle the good times well, but few handle the bad times as well as Cone. He wears the cloak of leadership because he's able to face the music and move on. David is also a loyal friend to players who've endured some rough times, including Darryl Strawberry.

I'm sure that David's qualities—grit, heart, and maturity—helped him to become only the sixteenth pitcher in major league history to pitch a perfect game. He performed this feat against the Montreal Expos on July 18, 1999, which happened to be my birthday. It was also Yogi Berra day at Yankee Stadium, with Yogi being honored before the game by many former Yankee greats, including Don Larsen, who pitched his historic perfect game in the 1956 World Series. The whole day was like magic from the start. Larsen threw out the game's first ball to Yogi, who handed it to catcher Joe Girardi. These Yankee legends, and 42,000 fans, then proceeded to witness Cone hurl his masterpiece, an 88-pitch gem in which he never once had a 3-ball count on a batter. He was helped by sparkling plays in the field by his teammates, including Girardi, Paul O'Neill, Scott Brosius, Ricky Ledee, and Chuck Knoblauch. David would be the first to say that he couldn't have done it without the support.

I've been fortunate to witness all three Yankee perfect games (I was a spectator at Larsen's, and manager for Wells's and Cone's). I couldn't have been happier for David, who had come awfully close to no-hitters before. The outpouring of celebration and affection for David in the aftermath of his accomplishment said a lot about how much people admire his character.

Many Yankees possess differing traits of leadership. Paul O'Neill is a warrior who wears his heart on his sleeve, inspiring others with his unrelenting determination. I've talked about Joe Girardi's willingnesss to sacrifice. But he also leads by example on the field. He gives every ounce of effort, both physically and mentally. Joe is articulate and extremely knowledgeable about the game—great material for a managerial career. Chili Davis is a consummate professional who goes about his business in such a mature way that his teammates look to him for leadership. Like Girardi, he takes time to mentor and support younger players. Bernie Williams is perhaps too low-key and introspective to be called a born leader, but players look up to him because he has so much dignity and grace, on and off the field. He also plays his heart out, every game.

In singling out these players, I don't mean to suggest that others on our club don't possess leadership qualities—many do. But each one mentioned represents a particular leadership trait you may be able to develop in your own work and personal life. Be humble enough to learn about leadership from the leaders in your midst.

The Team As Family

During the baseball season, players, coaches, and managers spend more time with each other than they do with their families. As a result, we often have the same intimacy, looseness, fun—and tension—of a typical family. When teams have good chemistry, the family model works in their favor. When the chemistry is off, it's not unlike a dysfunctional family.

I've experienced both. Obviously, with the Yankees we have the family model working in our favor. As far as I'm concerned, one characteristic of good families is the key to successful teams in sports and business: You don't have to get along all the time to work with and respect one another.

Isn't that the essence of a healthy family? Disagreements and tensions should not affect your love and commitment. The same holds true for a healthy team. You don't question your own loyalty just because you get angry at someone, just as you don't question their loyalty when they get mad at you. Straight communication is the most important key to the family model—get your feelings and concerns out in the open and move on.

Close colleagues on any team can adopt this philosophy. Expect smooth sailing at all times and you'll be pretty disappointed. Instead, build a level of respect, trust, and commitment that is so strong that your team can withstand the inevitable angers and tensions.

Your bonds should also enable you to withstand the winds of change. Every family undergoes changes that shake its foundation: Children are born, teenagers leave the house, financial crises arise. So, too, does every business: Employees leave, the power base shifts, people are downsized, the company restructures. Core members of the team need to retain that basic trust and cohesiveness—the family element—that allows them to survive and thrive no matter how much turbulence surrounds them.

You can also use the family as a model for accepting differences. Healthy families allow their members to be individuals, to grow and change. Loving family members don't reject one of their own for being different.

In every family or company, there will be people who are so individualistic that they cut against the grain. David Wells, who pitched for us in '97 and '98, was a good example. Boomer was a unique character with a wild, rebellious streak. When he first joined the team, his work habits left something to be desired. But we got a dialogue going, and in time he gave a much better effort. Boomer was accepted by the team despite his differences. Ultimately, he was embraced because of them.

During the 1998 off-season, it wasn't clear whether we'd be able to re-sign Bernie Williams. We made a pitch for Albert Belle, who consistently plays 160 games and puts up great offensive numbers. Many in the media speculated that Belle might be a disruption in our clubhouse. I was never concerned. First, it was hard to know the truth behind all the criticism about Albert. Second, I've always maintained that it's our job to be winners, not make friends. The fact that we have deep friendships is an advantage, not a necessity. You can't draw up blueprints for the kind of personalities you want on your team—it just doesn't work. Also, our group is so cohesive and professional that we feel we can handle any personality. We're not an impressionable club with young players who can be led down a primrose path by a disruptive individual.

Our first priority was to get Bernie Williams back, but if we couldn't, I was ready to consider Belle. I thought we should meet, so I flew down to Phoenix, where Albert and I played golf, then had dinner with his agent and our GM, Brian Cashman. Besides the fact that I wasn't happy with my golf game, it was an enjoyable day. I found Belle to be bright and personable, not the surly character that the media had depicted. He said he was looking forward to coming to Yankee Stadium, where he had always hit well. I was prepared to have him on our club. Albert asked for a certain dollar amount, and after running it by George, Cashman offered the money he was seeking. When Brian called to finalize the deal, Belle backed off. He did not say why he'd changed his mind, but we heard rumors that he was uncomfortable about the New York media.

Corporate teams should be able to deal with a wide range of personalities. I think it's a mistake to keep people off your team when you're overly concerned that they might not "fit in." When you are too exclusionary, you lose out on talent and diversity. You need a strong core group, but everyone doesn't have to fill your bill of particulars regarding the ideal teammate.

I've had only one player with the Yankees who was so difficult that he was a drag on the team. Ruben Sierra played for us in 1996, and he never understood the team concept. His first priority was playing time and personal statistics, that was it. Ruben would not understand why he was not in the lineup, and I spent chunks of time talking to him. I'd always be positive, put my arm around him, and explain my reasoning. No matter how hard I tried, Ruben never seemed to get it. After we traded him to Detroit in July, he thought he was ripping the Yankees when he said, "All they care about is winning."

Sierra was one of those rare cases where no amount of tolerance does any good. It happens in baseball, it happens in business, and it happens in families.

Managers shouldn't tolerate employees who are disruptive, but you do have to integrate people who are different. You can't condition your employees, in the name of teamwork, to think and behave alike. Strong leaders—and confident teammates—make room for people with quirks and different viewpoints, as long as they work hard and respect others. Leaders must also set an example for the team when it comes to accepting ethnic diversity. The Yankees are a remarkably diverse group, with guys from many ethnic and religious backgrounds. I'm proud of how well they get along. I like what Tino Martinez said about our 1998 pitching staff. "We have a pitcher from Cuba, a pitcher from Japan, and a pitcher from Panama. And we have Boomer, who is from Mars."

Communicating with players who speak little English is a challenge, but it's critical. I rely a great deal on my bilingual first-base coach, Jose Cardenal, who often acts as translator for Spanish-speaking players. Cardenal has enabled me to talk with pitcher Orlando "El Duque" Hernandez, who spoke almost no English when he defected from Cuba.

It was clear from the outset what El Duque needed in the way of communication. He was unfamiliar with many of our American baseball customs, and it was our job to describe how things work here without offending him. The first time I removed Hernandez from a ball game in the late innings, I went to the mound and he was reluctant to hand me the ball. I was confused, until he explained through Cardenal that this had never happened to him before. In Cuba, he'd always pitched until the game was over. We had to explain that in American ball, starters rarely finish games.

During our '98 Division Series against Texas, I had El Duque slotted as our fourth pitcher. But we won the series in three straight, so he didn't get the opportunity to pitch. Before we began the ALCS against Cleveland, I announced my starting rotation: Wells, Cone, Pettitte, Hernandez. El Duque made a comment to Cardenal to the effect, "Since I was next in line against Texas, aren't I supposed to be the first pitcher in the championship series?" Cardenal laughed and said "no," but El Duque really seemed to think that he should open the Cleveland series. We had to carefully explain our starting rotation system to El Duque to make certain he wasn't insulted.

With the help of his ever-present translator, George Rose, I've also been able to communicate with our Japanese pitcher, Hideki Irabu. It's not always easy to relate to him through a third person, but it's worth the effort. Managers should make every attempt to communicate with employees who don't speak fluent English. On one occasion, however, I wondered if my own efforts were all for naught. During our off-day workout before game six of the 1998 ALCS against Cleveland, I was standing behind the batting cage with Don Zimmer, and I looked down the right field line, where I saw two players standing together in the outfield. It was Hideki Irabu and El Duque Hernandez, chatting with each other—without translators. I poked Zimmer in the side. "Look at those guys," I said to Zim. "They're having a good old time. They're animated, they're laughing, and there's no interpreter out there. Looks like they've been playing us for fools." I still have no idea how these guys understood each other. While Zim and I got a kick out of the scene, it made me realize that any two people can find a way to connect if they're motivated and have common interests.

I must communicate with players who speak little or no English for practical reasons—to make sure they understand the team rules and game strategies. This may seem like a minor issue, but it represents my larger point—that we must be able to integrate everyone on our teams. Today's corporate world is more multi-ethnic and multicultural than ever before, so it behooves managers to get a dialogue going with team players from every conceivable background. I know from my experience with the Yankees just how worthwhile that effort can be.

For the most part, teams can and should be inclusive. When we tolerate differences in behavior and background, it makes us stronger. The family model is a powerful approach to teamwork. Our clubhouse is like a home—a place where we can get away from distractions, relax, and concentrate on our jobs. It helps, of course, that we enjoy our work. When you're a member of an organization working toward a shared dream, and you love your work and respect your teammates, you can't ask for much more. In my book, that makes you a winner already. The rings and rewards—they're just sweet desserts.

Torre's Winning Ways
Key #12: The Game of Life: Sacrifice Is Not Just a Bunt

- The qualities of leadership, steadiness, and commitment that lead to success often come from our families or other life experiences. Draw inspiration from all the positive role models in your past.

- **Sacrifice Is Not Just a Bunt**
  - Sacrifice builds character, and team players who sacrifice make it possible for organizations to thrive.
  - Workers and players on successful teams get rewarded in the end, if not with personal prizes then with team victories and career advancement.
  - Don't think of sacrifice as a nice-guy approach to winning approval from superiors. View it as a hard-nosed, smart way to succeed by lifting up yourself and your teammates at the same time.

- **Natural Born Leaders**
  - Many of us have leadership skills and don't know it. Leadership is based partly on personality, and partly on the twelve keys, including trust, respect, fairness, serenity, optimism, communication, and steadiness.
  - Ask yourself who in your work life—or among family, friends, or teachers—strikes you as being a great leader. Observe how they go about their

business, and put your finger on what makes them
inspiring.
* Be humble enough to learn about leadership from
the leaders in your midst.

* **The Team As Family**
  * The family model for organizations can work in
  your favor, if you focus on the positive values of
  intimacy, fun, and openness.
  * Build a level of respect, trust, and communication
  so strong that your team can withstand the
  inevitable angers and tensions.
  * Use the family model as a positive example for
  accepting differences—healthy families allow
  individuals to grow and change.
  * Know that the diversity of your team can be one of
  its great strengths.

About the Authors

JOE TORRE clinched his second World Series as the manager of the New York Yankees in 1998, making him the toast of New York and the baseball world. He has also managed and played for the Atlanta Braves, the New York Mets, and the St. Louis Cardinals, and he appeared in the All-Star Game nine times. He won Manager of the Year awards in both 1996 and 1998.

HENRY DREHER is a New York–based writer who specializes in health, psychology, and self-help. He has authored many books, as well as magazine articles and corporate speeches.